"Looking Back To M
by:
Flonzie Brown Wright

An Experience of **History & Hope**

Never let go of your Dream!

FBW & Associates, Incorporated
644 Elmwood Circle ~ Jackson, MS 39206
Bus. 601 981-8696~ Cell: 937-470-0627

Email: flonziebrownwright@att.net
"Exploring New Visions"

Website: flonziebrownwright.com

The book first published in 1994, is updated every five years.
FAST FORWARDS indicate significant and subsequent changes

The publishing team for this book includes the staff of:
FBW & Associates, Incorporated,
Rev. Dr. Jerrie L. Bascome McGill, cognos unlimited!
Dayton, Ohio,
and
Dr. Ethel W. Smith-Spencer, Smith-Spencer & Associates
Oakland, California

Graphics and cover design concept by:
Cynthia Goodloe Palmer & Brandon Thompson
Jackson, Mississippi

All photographs are from the personal archives of the Author
Photo on page 86 hangs in the New Civil Rights Museum
Jackson, Mississippi

Registration Questionnaire - a reprint from "Powerful Days,
The Civil Rights Photography of Charles Moore" (page 68)

Excerpts from "Ain't I A Woman," (page 100)
Credit to Abolitionist Sojourner Truth, 1851

Cover photos: Election Card—1968, Second photo, 1999

~Dedication~

This book is lovingly dedicated to my Parents:

Mr. Frank Brown, Sr.
1916 – 2006

Mrs. Littie Dawson Brown
1921 - 2011

And Both Brothers:

Sydney J. Brown, Sr.
1940 – 2009

Frank L. Brown, Jr.
1948—2013

Because of who they were, I am!
Many Special Memories.

A Special Tribute to my son Edward:
A Second Generation Trailblazer

April 7, 1960 ~ March 6, 2014

We moved to Jackson from Canton in 1974, my second child Edward, Jr., was 13. After several unsuccessful attempts by him to play softball at the neighborhood Lake Hico Park, I was required to file a lawsuit on his behalf against the Mayor and the City of Jackson. This resulted in the Lake Hico Park now being opened to all residents.

In 2012, Councilman Chokwe Antar Lumumba, (now also deceased), introduced a Resolution to the Jackson City Council commending the bravery of my young thirteen year old son and presented him with a special Commendation.

Pictured along with the Councilman are the following family members: (*left to right), Mom, Ed, Debra (wife), Kathy (daughter), Cynthia (sister) and Gacobie (son).*

In the spring of 2013, then Mayor Lumumba

and the entire City Council agreed to designate a special space in the Lake Hico Park as the "***Edward Goodloe, Jr., Walking Trail.***" I am grateful that Ed had the opportunity to live to see his bravery come full circle.

These two great men used their God-given "space" to make a difference for the masses. The Mayor used his training and political influence to serve others. Edward used his love of family and community to open up a recreational facility for thousands to enjoy daily. I'm proud of each one as 21st Century Trailblazers!

November 2013

Table of Contents

About Flonzie

Flonzie B. Brown-Wright, is the second child born in Farmhaven, Mississippi to Mr. and Mrs. Frank Brown, Sr. Her family has lived in Canton, Mississippi since 1948. Farmhaven is approximately 16 miles east of Canton, where her parents and both brothers, now deceased, lived for a number of years.

She was educated in the private and public schools in Canton, Mississippi. She received a Fain Fellowship and attended Tougaloo College in Tougaloo, Mississippi. Her concentration was Political Science, Pre-Law and Black History. In 1964, she was granted advanced administrative training through the National Office of the NAACP in New York City, New York. She served the Millsaps College in Jackson, Mississippi as Co-founder and Vice-President of the Institute of Politics. **_Fast Forward_**: In 2018, she was the recipient of an honorary degree, the Doctor of Humane Letters from Tougaloo College, Tougaloo, MS, and special honors from LaMoyne College in Syracuse, NY. Her employment and professional career has spread from the dusty roads of Mississippi to the White House as she interacted with many individuals' of local, national and international prominence. She was commissioned by the Equal Employment Opportunity Commission (EEOC), in 1964 as an Investigator of employment discrimination complaints. She served as President of AFGE/EEO AFL-CIO Union, Local 3599 for more than twelve (12) years where she supervised an eight state, thirteen city and 600 employee region. She retired from the EEOC in 1989 at which time she received among her many awards, "The Chairman's' Special Award for Outstanding Service."

While living in Mississippi, her activism began in the early 1960's, specializing in grass-roots organizing. She has used every available opportunity to share with others what she learned through these valued experiences. In 1989, she married William Russell Wright, Sr. They resided in Germantown, Ohio for almost 22 years until her return to Mississippi to care for her parents and younger brother. One of the gems of their marriage was parenting a blended family of 7 biological and 3 foster children, 20 plus grandchildren and 4 great grandchildren.

She continues to spend her time sharing the history of our ancestors by teaching, lecturing and speaking on a myriad of historical issues.

Credits, Memberships and Honors

President and CEO, FBW & Associates, Incorporated, 1994
Founder, The Flonzie B. Wright Scholarship Foundation, 1994
Member, NCNW, NAACP, SCLC, 1960's & continuing
Board President, National Caucus and Center for the Black Aged, Jackson, MS, 1984
(The lobby in the facility dedicated in 1985 bears her name as The Flonzie B. Goodloe Lobby)
Founding Member/President, Women for Progress, Inc., Jackson, MS, 1978
Charter Member, Bethune Day Care Center, Canton, MS, 1966
Founder, the Vernon Dahmer Youth Singers for Freedom, 1966
Production Advisor, ZDF West Germany Television, Inc., 1970
(This collaboration produced five (5) documentaries)
Recipient, "The Wyche Fowler Congressional Citation", Atlanta, GA, 1985
Vice-President Emeritus, NCEEOC Locals #216, New York, NY, 1989
President, AFGE Local 3599, Jackson, MS, 1990
Recruitment Consultant, Montgomery County Children Services, Dayton, OH
Founder, "Yes, We Care" Foster-care Recruitment Committee, Dayton, OH, 1990
Listed in Who's Who Among African Americans, 2003
Lecturer and Motivational Speaker for Elementary, High School, Colleges,
Universities and Community Organizations—50 plus years & continuing
Writer, "Straight From The Heart" – A Multi-Western Newspaper Collaborative, 1991—1992
Member, New Hope Baptist Church, Jackson, MS, 2010
Consultant, SCLC/WOMEN's Nationals AIDS Awareness Program, Dayton, OH, 1990
Guest-Co-host, "Expressions" – WDAO Radio, Dayton, OH, 1992
Co-founder of "What About Tomorrow" Women's Fellowship, Dayton, OH, 1994
Writer, "It's Prayer Time" for Mrs. Mamie Clemons, Pittsburgh, PA, 2005
Co-Writer, "Together We Hurt, Together We Heal" for Donnis F. Johnson, 2008
Executive Video Producer, "And Before I'll Be Your Slave", 1995
Best Selling Author, "Looking Back To Move Ahead", 1994
Collaborator, "Standing On My Sisters' Shoulders" Video Documentary, 1997
Consultant, Victoria Theatre, Dayton, OH, 1995
Consultant/Author "But For The Drugs" Initiative for Project **CURE**, Dayton, 1990
Member, Professional Women's Association, Washington, DC, 1998
Recipient of more than 450 Local, State, National, Church & Community Service Awards
Ohio State Certified, AIDS Awareness Trainer, Dayton, OH, 1992
Featured – Purpose Magazine, Martin Luther King Special Edition, 1993
Featured – Canton, Mississippi Civil Rights Documentary, 2000
Featured – Tomorrow's Mississippi – Tomorrow's South, September, 1999
Honored – John F. Kennedy Center for the Performing Arts, 1993
Recipient, Drum Major for Justice Award, SCLC, Dayton, OH, 1994
Student Affairs Scholar in Residence— Miami University at Middletown, OH, 2006-2010
Honored – "Phenomenally She" Outstanding African American Women, Jackson, MS, 2006
Producer - "Standing Tall in Tough Times" Video Documentary, 2006
Listed – Who's Who Among Black Mississippians, 2010
Co-Event Director – Return of the Mississippi 50th Freedom Riders Reunion, 2011
Recipient - Special Honors – 100 Black Men of Starkville, MS, 2012
Honored – Drum Major for Justice Award/American Assoc. for Affirmative Action, 2011
Featured as one of Mississippi's Outstanding Women in Civil Rights Exhibit, 2008
(Smith Robertson Cultural Museum)
Recipient – Fannie Lou Hamer Humanitarian Award, 2012
Recipient – HOPE Award for Social Justice, New Hope Baptist Church, Jackson, MS, 2012
Honored - Naming of Court Room in Canton, MS City Hall, 2016
Graduate—FBI Citizens Academy, Jackson, MS, 2016
Honored – by the National FBI in Washington, DC, with Directors Award, 2017
Featured—*Two Mississippi Museums, the Civil Rights Gallery , 2017*
Featured on Cover - Mississippi Christian Living, January 2018 Edition
Honored by the Mississippi State Senate, the House of Representatives and the
Women of the House of Representatives, 2018
Recipient—Honorary Degree—the Doctor of Humane Letters, Tougaloo College, MS, 2018
Honored by Christian Women United, 2018
Recipient—the Dr. Amelia Boynton Robinson Award, Tuskegee, AL. 2018

Foreword

Ethel and Flonzie, 1994

What makes a book? The living, the dreams, the struggles, the emotions, the fears, the courage and hopes of all mankind make a book. Flonzie Brown-Wright has certainly lived and made a book. As you read this book, you will understand the type of person whose life has been book worthy. This book chronicles the life of Flonzie as she has made a footprint in the sands of time. Her childhood remembrances and motivations are conveyed, and the significance of each achievement along the way.

Aside from the threats and fears of earlier years, the discrimination, segregation, intimidation and degradation no longer plague our people to the same degree of the past, thanks to her efforts. Flonzie risked everything to make a difference, and she did. Not content merely to accept the status quo of the times, she refused to allow the status quo to control her thoughts, feelings and actions. Her desire for equality was a driving force that helped her overcome the struggle against the odds.

My cousin, Flonzie, has continued to grow and contribute to civic affairs wherever she chooses to reside. She has much to offer her community. She is one of the most unselfish persons that I know. I have watched her interact with people of all walks of life. She inspires by example, encourages by suggestion and motivates by her energetic persona. The importance of her contributions can be measured only by the successes accomplished. As this book so adequately points out, Flonzie Brown Wright is a woman of unusual courage, and it shows.

Ethel W. Spencer-Smith, Ph.D.
Spencer-Smith and Associates, Oakland, California

Preface

Since the early 1960's, I have felt compelled to share many of my personal experiences while growing up in a small rural Mississippi town. It is my desire that the reader will walk with me as we revisit the many events which occurred during the civil rights days of the movement. I hope that this first-hand view will assist you, and others, in better understanding this compelling need.

Canton, Mississippi has so much rich history, so much to write and talk about, so much to understand and appreciate. As we look back for the purpose of moving ahead, it is my hope that this book will encourage our youth and will serve to validate the involvement of those unrecognized heroes and sheroes.

As we experience life, good times, some not so good, it is important to understand that looking back is healthy if it allows one to build upon those experiences. *Moving Ahead* should be the positive manifestation of *Looking Back.*

By no means do I proclaim myself as an Author in an authentic sense, I do believe, however, that when God has given one a mission and a message, one must accept the mission and "Just Do It." The message must be told. When one has been given a talent, it must be used for the betterment of mankind or one will be held accountable.

From my youth, I have always believed that I was endowed with a special gift from God, a gift that has taken me to heights that I could not have imagined or reached had it not been for His kindness and mercy.

For who I am and ever hope to be, I owe it all to God first, Mom and Dad, both brothers, my children, extended family, dear friends, my corporate community and my husband, Bill.

A portion of the proceeds from the book continues to be used to maintain *"The Flonzie B. Wright Scholarship Foundation", a 501(c)(3) Tax Exempt Organization.* My vision is to provide an opportunity for young people to receive a better education. If this fund helps just one child or several children, these efforts would have been worth it all.

Acknowledgements

Cynthia Verneatta Goodloe Palmer

Memories: *Like The Corners of My Mind....*
Misty Watered Colored Memories, of the Way We Were!

As far back as I can remember, my mom was always 28. Why, because people often said to me, "You sure have a young looking mom, how old is she?" I'd always respond, 28. It seems as if for years, my response was always, 28.

My mother has been the most positive influence in my life and still remains. She has been a wealth of knowledge, a source of strength, a great inspiration, and a lot of fun. She has been a teacher, a doctor, a counselor, an instructor, a chauffeur, a banker, a caring and loving mom.

There are some lasting things that I remember the most. One such thought is our first apartment in Canton, Mississippi. It was a new and small two bedroom apartment. I slept with my mom. My brothers slept in bunk beds in their very own room.

One day, someone gave us a cat. She tipped in and out of the apartment until finally she delivered a family of her own. We cared for the kittens as if they were real children. We fed them, played with them, put them down for their naps and tucked them into their "boxes" at night.

I remember our first home. Again, I slept with my mom. This was a nice, little, cozy home. After a while, my mom decided to add two rooms so that I could have my very own bedroom.

Along came our first dog..., Fu Fu. One day Fu Fu was hit by a car and left in a ditch to die. Being the caring person that my mom is, she picked Fu Fu up out of the ditch and took her to the doctor. Lo and behold, Fu Fu came back with a crutch taped to her broken leg. I had never seen a dog with a crutch before. Mom could have insisted that the dog be put to sleep, but she didn't. She used this experience to teach us the value of life, even for a pet.

Now remember, mom is still 28, that is to me of course. When my mom ran for political office, I felt as if I ran for political office also. I traveled with mom to many meetings, rallies and other campaign activities. As a result of her hard work, she was the first Black Female elected to public office in the bi-racial town of Canton, Mississippi, pre or post reconstruction. Being involved with mom in the community was as important to me as it was to her.

In the late 60's, our home was filled with white students from LaMoyne College in Syracuse, New York. These students came to help further the cause of "freedom". You see, mom never taught us any distinction between white and Black. Never have I heard her express anything other than we were all equal. Back in the 60's, that type of attitude was not an everyday occurrence. That experience emphasized mom's teachings that all of God's children were created equal.

I remember my first spanking. One day after school, I decided to stop by and visit Aunt Jo and Uncle Sydney. I made this decision in spite of mom's instructions, to always come straight home from school or get her permission first to do otherwise. It was important to mom to know where we were at all times. Upon returning home, my mom was so kind that she allowed Grandmother *Littie* to do the spanking. My brother Edward also remembers the "kind, flowing" touch that mom administered to him when he too was disobedient.

I was unaware that mom's life as well as ours had been threatened by the Ku Klux Klan. This was her way of protecting us. We did not know that she followed us home each day after school on another street to ensure that we arrived safely. I remember the Sunday morning my brother Darrell was born. Cousin Lizette, a mid-wife, came to my grandparent's home with a big brown paper bag. I was told my mom's baby was in the paper bag. This was a joyous occasion for us. As I learned to care for Darrell, I was being groomed to care for my own children one day.

My first job was secured by mom where I worked with her as a gift wrapper during the Christmas season. I was twelve years old at that time. It was necessary for mom to work a second and sometimes a third job, because she was the primary provider for her three children. Later on, I remember buying my first stereo and opening up my very own charge account in my name. Mom knew that as I discovered Visa, Discover and Master Cards, etc., she wanted me to be prepared to manage my finances as I grew to become a homemaker. Of course, she was still 28.

I've watched my mom grow up to be the woman she is today. She continues to strive for excellence and believes in being the best she can be. She instilled in us that same zeal for excellence.

Mom has given me a sense of direction about my life. She has always exhibited a sense of confidence and positiveness. She has been a perfect example of a good role model for any child to follow. As I am now an adult, there is no one that I wish to emulate other than my mom. She taught us so many positive life lessons and still does.

I salute mom for undertaking this project. In writing this book, she is sharing a very special part of herself. I am excited about her vision for the *Scholarship Foundation.* This effort will assist in developing strong children for the future. Edward, Jr., Darrell and I appreciate the opportunity to share in our mom's dreams and aspirations with you. I hope as you read this book, you will grasp the vision of *"Looking Back To Move Ahead."*

Lovingly ~ Your Daughter,

Cynthia

Acknowledgements continue

Mrs. Annie Devine

I have known Flonzie since she was a young child. She, my daughter Monette and girlfriend Mamie, were all best friends as little girls growing up. I often watched them as they gleefully played together. I am pleased to have had the opportunity to watch each of them grow up to be women of purpose and women of responsibility. I often wondered what these three little "pip squeaks" would become. I am happy to say that I am proud of each of them.

As I watched Flonzie evolve into the courageous woman that she is today, I am honored to say that I knew this youngster when...,I am also pleased to acknowledge that perhaps I may have had some influence on her political career.

As the civil rights movement swung into high gear in Canton, the community was seeking someone who we could encourage to run for Election Commissioner.

She was granted advanced administrative training through the National Office of the NAACP in New York City, New York.

We needed someone who would be fair to all of the citizens. We knew that in order to get a first-hand grasp of the multiplicity of election and voting problems, these elements were essential.

Over and over again, Flonzie's name kept coming to mind. Finally, I approached her about running for this position. She gave me a hard time, using every excuse she could find as to why she was not the one for this position. After some time, she finally became convinced that the community was serious and wanted her in that position. She consented to run for this position and became our first Black Female elected to a public office in Canton/Madison County, Mississippi post or pre-reconstruction.

She has done much for this community, while in office and as a private citizen. She brought to the Election Commissioners' position a sense of dignity, a sense of purpose, a sense of honesty, fairness and equality.

Her election has forever changed the political climate in Canton as well as the state of Mississippi.

We are proud of her many accomplishments. The trust that this community placed in her in the 1960's remains in tact to this day. She has not disappointed us. We commend her in this selfless endeavor as she tells the story about our hometown of Canton, Mississippi.

To Flonzie with love,
Mrs. Annie Devine
(Mother "D")

My Wife, A Special Lady

I met Flonzie in April of 1989. I knew when we met that she was a special lady and I wanted her to be a part of my life. On December 17th of that same year, we were married.

During the course of our marriage, our expectations of each other have far surpassed our dreams.

My wife is a tremendous lady. Having had the opportunity to visit her hometown of Canton, I have seen many pleasant surprises. Being born and raised in Ohio, I have to admit that many of my perceptions of Mississippi were somewhat negative. Over the years of our marriage, I am happy to say, without a doubt, that many of my feelings have changed. I have witnessed first-hand the New South that Flonzie has spoken about so affectionately.

Based on what I perceived and what I've seen, many positive changes have taken place in her home state of Mississippi.

I am proud to be married to this courageous woman who has held high her vision of her hometown.

Having met many of her friends, I am grateful for the love they have shown to both of us. It is with love, admiration and respect that I commend her courage in facing the many challenges as she lived the "southern experience."

She shares her gifts and talents without expecting anything in return. As God blesses her, she exhibits a special air of excitement as she shares those blessings with others.

My gratitude is extended to those who know Flonzie and have encouraged her to become this great lady.

I am honored to have become a valued part of Flonzie's loving family.

William and Flonzie, 1990

Editor's Corner

by

Rev. Jerrie L. Bascome McGill, Ph.D.

Superintendent of Dayton Public Schools

Dayton, Ohio

My yes to Flonzie's initial call for editorial assistance was given without hesitation. I continue to be grateful to this wonderful, energetic and prayer-filled lady for provid-ing me the opportunity to participate in this great adventure. I am grateful to two wonderful friends for sitting with us in the final stages to ensure the presence of the elements of clarity and whose energies helped sharpen our focus in *Looking Back to Move Ahead.*

Flonzie's work and achievements in the Mississippi civil rights movement are amply documented. The significance of this book is that it gives a face and a name to one of the many unsung heroes and she-roes of the movement who, for the most part, were unknown and whose contributions were not widely celebrated. The publication provides a window into the reality of the experiences not only for Flonzie, but also of the men and women who were a part of the panorama of her life and who were actively engaged in the struggle.

Prior to this work, the details about Black citizens attaining success in the voter registration process were not as widely known. Prior to this work, specific information about the behaviors of local elected officials and local citizens, committed to using arbitrary and/or violent means to preserve an archaic and entrenched system, continued to be relayed through fictionalized accounts. The recounted experiences of Flonzie and her friends, colleagues and co-workers answer the question: "What was life really like for the countless men, women and children who lived everyday in the midst of upheaval and remained committed to their freedom?" Thanks to Flonzie, we no longer have to pose that question.

I am pleased for Flonzie. I am thankful that she chose me to walk with her as she was challenged with the many responsibilities and requirements associated with the completion of this project. I only wish her well.

Part I

Looking Back

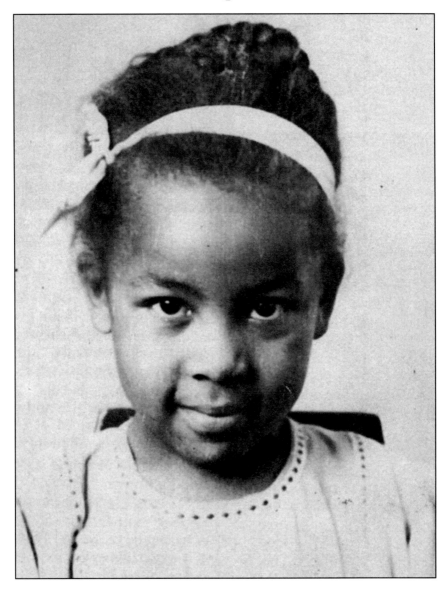

Flonzie's first school day picture at age 5

Chapter 1

A Long Way Back

On the day of my birth, August 12, 1942, my parents, Mr. and Mrs. Frank Brown, Sr., had their prayers answered. They had their baby girl. They could not have been more proud. My aunts and uncles, Grandpa Bozie, other relatives and friends came to welcome me and to celebrate my arrival. My older brother Syd, was less than two years old when I was born. From what I am told, he was ready to play big brother. As time went on and my younger brother Frank, Jr., was born, I was ready to play big sister to him. We lived in Farmhaven, a small rural farming community between Canton and Carthage, Mississippi. This was and remains one of those areas predominately owned by Blacks.

Due to both of their deaths, I was not privileged to know either of my grandmothers. My dad's mom was named Frances. I am named for my mom's mom, a descendant of the Muscogee Creek Indian Nation. Both grandfathers impacted my life. Papa Bozie, my mom's dad, was a tall giant of a man of African, Indian and Caucasian heritage. While he stood tall in stature, he stood taller in principles. He was a very smart man and did not accept the "sharecropping syndrome" as a way of life. He was very independent. He leased his land, owned livestock and made a good living for his family. My dad's father, Papa Rob, dug graves, dressed hogs and made molasses for many surrounding communities. At an early age he lost his hearing, but could understand anything that was said to him. He intently watched facial expressions. He was not a learned man by educational standards; but was endowed with old fashioned mother-wit. He was a successful businessman who lived until the ripe old age of eighty-eight. At that age he was still making molasses and showing others the skills of the molasses-making trade. His tenacious spirit encouraged each of their 12 children to also become self-employed, and they all were, even in the challenging 1950's. He was determined to lead by example.

I remember so well as a child being visited and nurtured by both grandpas. Papa Bozie, a learned Bible scholar, used to tell me Bible stories from the time I can remember. He told me all about Moses and how Joshua "fit" the Battle of Jericho, about Job and his patience and about Jesus, the Christ child. He would then pick up his guitar and sing songs to my brother and me. He died when I was twelve, but I never forgot this towering giant.

Growing up, Syd and I were inseparable. His first day at school was just as traumatic for him as it was for me. We both cried at day. He was five and I was four. For the first time, we were separated.

The trauma was so bad that Mother asked the teacher if I could come to school just to be with my "Bubba." She readily agreed, because she was also our Sunday School teacher and felt that my parents were doing, as she used to say, "a good job in raising us."

After being in school for a couple of days, I began to learn along with the older children; and after a month, I was studying at the same grade level as the first grade students. I was now, officially, in the first grade at the age of four. I could not believe it. Our school was an old fashioned one room, built on the back of a church where all 8 grades were gathered in the same room and taught by one teacher. I remember the big black pot-bellied stove, the wood pile in the comer of the room, the homemade rack for our coats and the table for our lunches. There were not enough desks for each  of us to have our own. Our teacher, Mrs. Lillie Pickett, was very kind and allowed some of us to study at her desk or on a homemade table.

Throughout the day, especially during the winter months, men from the community would come to check on the stove. They took pleasure in seeing that it was filled with wood. They believed this to be a "man's job." The blackboard was an old wooden door that my dad painted black. Mrs. Pickett was ever so creative and used every opportunity to improvise so that we would get the benefit of her knowledge and creativity. She loved each of us in a very special way and always had time to listen to each of our questions. We would come to her, one after another, with our scraped knees, runny noses or broken pencils. What was a series of crises for us, was an everyday occurrence for Mrs. Pickett.

There was no such thing as integrated schools which would have provided an opportunity for an equal education for all children, including poor and Black children. The books from which we studied were books that had been transported from Michigan, Tennessee and from wherever Mrs. Pickett could get them from. They were overly used, marked up and had worn out covers. Our teacher made an effort to erase as much of the scribbling as she could. Mrs. Pickett taught us how to cover our books using either brown paper bags, Christmas wrapping paper or left over wall paper scraps, provided by the women of the church and community.

There were no school buses, so each day we walked back and forth to school, in the sun, in the cold, in the rain, muddy roads and all. Luckily, the school was not that far and Syd and I walked along with our schoolmates. Mom watched us as we left for school everyday, and waited for us in the afternoon. Because of her love for us, some mornings, she would walk us part of the way to school.

Mom would meet us at the bridge and return with us in the afternoon. Not that she was afraid that we would be kidnapped or harmed; this was the manifestation of the love that she taught and shared.

During some of that time my dad was out of town working on what is now known as the Natchez Trace which covers 444 miles in three states. Mom did not work. There were few employment opportunities for rural Black women. The only work choices at that time were housekeeping for folks in the **"BIG"** house," going to the cotton field or staying home. Mom elected to stay home and give her children all the tender, loving care that she could. Things were tight, but Mom always had a remarkable way of "stretching the eyeballs" off of a dollar bill, even so today.

Grandmother Flonzie died when Mom and her siblings were quite young.

Aunt Tommie, Grandmother Flonzie's sister and her husband Uncle Gus, provided nurturance and guidance to Mom, her sisters and her brothers. They also lived in the Farmhaven community and often brought sweet potatoes, meat and a variety of vegetables to them. The extended family love concept was manifested as they assisted in their rearing. Mom's youngest sister, Aunt Bertha, her baby son John, and two younger brothers came to live with us. I became like a daughter to Aunt Bertha.

Aunt Bertha   She'd comb my hair and starch and ironed my dresses. She often shared how she'd slip and re-iron my dresses because, according to her, Mom didn't put enough starch in them. She and Syd were pals also. Everyday, she'd dress us twice daily. Over the years, even though we respected her as our aunt, she became like a big sister to us.

At each phase of my life, my parents, my aunts, my neighbors, my teachers and my grandfathers, taught me to do my best and to help others to help themselves. As I grew older, the significance of their teachings became more evident.

Syd and I have never lost our closeness. As we grew, so did our love and respect for each other. Today as I observe him, I see him implementing many of the "fireside" values taught to us by mom, dad and extended family members.

Flonzie at age 4, Syd at age 5

He really is the best brother a sister could have or wish for.

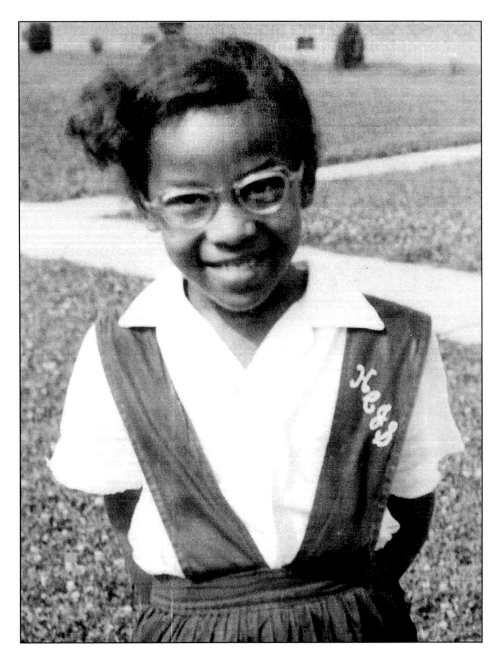

Flonzie at 8 years old, and a student at the
Holy Child Jesus Catholic School, Canton, MS

Chapter 2

Reflections of The Days When

In 1948, when I was six years old, my parents moved to Canton, which was considered the Mecca for surrounding communities. There were restaurants, cafés, barber shops, movie theaters, department stores, drug stores, several local banks, city schools, doctors' offices and other businesses to serve the more than twenty thousand residents. Even though Madison County was predominately Black, our people did not own "their fair share." They owned very little. Most jobs held by Blacks were menial. They worked as housekeepers, cooks, day laborers or field workers. Poverty in the Black neighborhoods, in comparison to that in the white neighborhoods, was overwhelmingly out of proportion. While there have been many strides and gains made since my childhood, poverty must now be redefined.

That same year my younger brother, Frank, Jr., was born. Mom has yet to tell me her secret as to how Frank, Jr., and I were both born on the same day, August 12th, six years apart. Not only that, all of us kids were born on the 12th of the month. Syd's birthday is December 12th.

Our first house in Canton was a little three room "shot gun" house in Hickory Alley. This newly developed subdivision was owned by one of the white businessmen. Rent was cheap, but the home was comfortable. Mom, with her sewing skills, made the curtains and quilts and decorated our home using her gifts of softness and creativity. Bubba and I attended the only Black school. In Canton, as in all places throughout the deep south, Blacks attended their own schools, whites attended theirs. At the age of six, I knew absolutely nothing about segregation, or about the effects of racism. Even as we grew older, Mom and Dad made a concerted effort to shield us from the ugliness of racism and inferiority as a mind-set or what our value-system could be.

For two years, we attended Cameron Street School, which housed all 12 grades. In our first year, I had to be re-assigned to the first grade because of the school system's age/grade requirement. My new school did not recognize my second grade status at age six. Even though mother questioned the re-assignment, school policies did not honor my grade status. Having to be put back a grade made me even more determined to keep up with my studies and to excel in all of my studies.

I was so excited to be in a large school, in a single classroom, with one teacher and my age mates. It was that opportunity plus previous teachings which allowed me to excel above some of my classmates.

.

Being smart in my studies did not go over well with some of my classmates. I believe also their disdain of me was due to me being very fair-skinned and the way mom dressed me. Mom styled my hair with my very own long blondish braids. All of those things did not help either.

Some of the kids bullied me and made fun of me, they often called me "that old red girl, with that red hair." They continued by saying said, "Her daddy must have been a white man!" Quite the contrary, however, that was still very hurtful. My mom could have *passed* for a white woman. She still can. My dad is a dark-skinned distinguished looking man who is proud to be who and what he is. Classmates pulled my braids as Mother always dressed me with those big fluffy matching ribbons and matching socks. They threw dirt on the dresses that Mom had so lovingly made. I did not understand these cruel acts and ugly comments by my class mates. It was not until my college years that I truly understood this type of thinking, which emanated from the caste struggle, during the post slavery era. I'm sure; these were well intentioned kids as many of them became lifetime friends. The three of us children were reared differently with different priorities and expectations. The long lasting result of these hurtful experiences was an aversion to even wearing the color red until my my late forties.

Now the school books were another issue. Our books were used, many were tattered and most were just plain ragged. These books came from the local white schools. Any given book may have already been used by up to ten white students. By the time we got them, much of the subject matter was old and outdated. As I later learned, that was the plan.

Each year at Cameron Street School, we were allowed to participate in a play. That was fun. We decorated the gym with crepe paper and other decorations to help fulfill the theme of the play. With much excitement and anticipation, we sang our songs, did our dances, said our speeches and talked about our involvement for months. Our parents and other community people came to see these much talked about "productions."

After about a year, we moved to another neighborhood. My parents' friends, Mr. & Mrs. Earnest Garrett, (African Americans), actually owned several houses. We moved into one of them. It had the same amenities, three rooms this time with indoor plumbing. The two of us, Syd and I, continued to attend the same public school.

In 1946, a Catholic mission and school were founded, established for Canton's Black children. I was seven years of age. This Mission was run by nuns from the *Order of the Franciscan Sisters of Perpetual Adoration, FSPA,* headquartered in LaCrosse, Wisconsin. None of us knew what to think with their long black strange looking clothes with nothing visible but the roundness of their faces. Their primary goal was to establish a full-fledged Mission/church with recreational activities.

My first piano recital at age eight at Holy Child. My younger brother Frank, Jr., gave me these flowers from one of mom's many flower gardens. He was very proud of his "big sis." We share the same birthday, August 12th.

The nuns opened a little second-hand store so that the people they served could buy affordable clothes. Because they had a national networking system, they were able to get clothing, household and other items at nominal cost to the families in the community. The nuns actively canvassed the area and recruited students and families to understand their mission and to be a part of their movement. Even though the mission still exists today, it is operated by local residents.

In 1950, at almost age eight, I enrolled in the Holy Child Jesus Mission School as a fourth grade student. Even though many of our books had been used by other Catholic students in other states, the quality of the lessons was on a much higher instructional level. The school began with approximately seventy (70) students from grades one to six. The highest average reading grade level for all the 70 students was about 1.5. The nuns took such a personal interest in each of us that on a rotating basis, we stayed after school for special tutoring. Even on Saturdays, they scheduled time for us to come and read, to study math and other subjects in which we were deficient. Those who were strong in certain subjects, helped others as we organized study teams.

One of my mom's dreams for me was that I learn to play the piano. One of the nuns, Sister Vincenza, gave me music lessons so that this dream could be realized. I must have taken music all of the years that I was a student at Holy Child. So many lasting friendships were cultivated during my years at Holy Child Jesus School. I was trained in many fundamental areas which prepared me for many experiences yet to come. Later, I used musical arts to earn extra money for my children.

I fondly remember Bertha Bowman, one of the 70 students. She became my inspiration and my dear friend. Bertha and I promised that we were going to both become nuns. We studied the Catechism together everyday. We wore long scarves on our heads mimicking the nuns. We went to the rectory daily after school just to be in their presence. We knew the rosary and adopted many of the practices of the Catholic Church. At the tender age of 15, Bertha left Canton to enter the convent and to pursue her calling. Her parents and so many including myself, were heartbroken beyond words to see her leave. Bertha later took the name, Sister Thea Bowman, in honor of her father, Dr. Theon E. Bowman. My mom was convinced that at age twelve, I was not prepared to make that same life-changing decision, even though I thought I was. Sister Thea and I remained in touch throughout the years, even during her illness and death. Like Thea, I have always tried to remain a servant.

In Canton, with much excitement, we watched her go through various phases of her "sisterhood" and we could not have been more proud of her. I've often wondered what my life would have been like had I too became a Catholic nun.

At her request, it was my honor to sing the song, "Zion's Hill" at her Eulogistical Celebration in April 1990. What a celebration it was. This song, sang many times by Mr. Earnest Garrett, was special to her because she sang it at her mom and dad's services. Thea planned all of the details of her own service. So many people came from all parts of the world. Because of the huge crowd, the final service had to be moved to the largest Cathedral in Jackson. Through her suffering and death, she taught many what love was.

I treasure the memories of my many visits with her prior to her death. She had a remarkable way of healing others as she lay stricken with cancer. Your intent may have been to encourage her, but without a doubt, your visit ended with her encouraging you.

She remains one of my greatest inspirations. Because of her decision to become a nun, many people have been able to better identify their own personal mission and purpose. I am proud to be one of those whose life continues to be impacted by her life and death.

Sister Thea Bowman, FSPA
1937—1990
Official Dedicatory Portrait by Artist, Marshall Bouldin, 1988
She sent this photo to me while I was still residing in Germantown, Ohio

Chapter 3

To My Parents ~ With Love

Mr. and Mrs. Frank Brown, Sr., 1988

The summer of my tenth birthday was an exciting time. Like all little girls, I found new girlfriends. We were full of the giggles and talked "girl talk". I was excited about my new school clothes. I was on top of the world. Summer quickly drew to a close, it was time to turn my attention to school. Playtime was over, it was time for serious business.

In Mississippi, school always began in early September; the weather was still warm. My new girlfriends and I walked home from school together each afternoon. We easily spent an hour walking back and forth to each other's homes, chatting and giggling all the way.

Educational opportunities for Blacks were very limited in the South in the 20's, 30's, 40's and 50's. My parents, being mindful of this, made a concerted effort to provide my brothers and me with the best education they could afford. Dad was a plumber for a local white businessman. Mom stayed home as a homemaker and seamstress. They continued the tradition of their parents who instilled in them a desire for achievement.

Both my parents graduated from the eighth grade. For Black students in the rural deep South, this was as high as they could go, because there were no neighborhood schools which provided them a higher education.

In many rural areas, Black children could only attend school four months out of a year; the remainder of the time was spent in the fields as sharecroppers. Their years in school occurred well before <u>Brown vs. The Board of Education, in 1954.</u> This landmark decision mandated equal educational opportunities for all children, regardless of their race.

On a late September day in 1952, my girlfriends and I were walking home from school in our usual giggly manner when a car driven by a lone white woman pulled up to the curb. She called out of the window, "You, little girl, come here."

We all looked at each other with uncertainty. We were dressed in our school uniforms, so we all looked somewhat alike. One of the girls asked, "Mam, who do you want?" She replied, "You, the little girl *with the long braids* and ribbons in your hair."

It became evident that she was talking to me. Mom insisted that I look a certain way each day. At ten, I was beginning to think differently, but she relished the idea that her little girl had to wear braids, ribbons and matching socks on a daily basis. I went to the lady's car and asked, "Yes, ma'am?" She asked my name, where I lived, who my folks were, how old was I and other informational details about me.

I answered her questions as I had been taught--in a courteous manner. I did not see her as a white woman. In my family, we were not taught to see a distinction between the races. My grandfather's father, was a white man. Relatives, both Black and white, lived near by. We all knew each other and interacted regularly. Since I was also accustomed to being taught by white nuns, I did not see this incident as a racial one.

After I satisfactorily answered her questions, she stated: *"I have two children and I would like for you to babysit in the afternoons and on Saturdays."* She gave me her telephone number and address and I promised to be at her home the next afternoon, after getting mom's permission, of course, which I did not think would be a problem.

Without giving this matter a thought, I was elated, <u>I was going to have a "good" job.</u>" I was so excited. I could not wait to get home to tell Mom the good news. Most of my friends had evening, week-end and summer jobs; now I had one. After finding mom, (sewing of course), I told her that, "I was now employed for Mrs. Ann", (that was really her name). Mom replied with great fervor, "You cannot do that". I thought to myself, "Huh, I'm ten years old, why can't I babysit for that nice lady?"

Mom must have read my mind. She replied again this time quite emphatically, with her hands on her hips, and with her finger pointing directly at me, she exclaimed, almost screaming, **"Understand me well, You Cannot Do That!!"**

She gave no other explanation at that time, however, I knew better than to continue my lawyer-like interrogation of "Mrs. Little", as she was and continues to be fondly called. Oh, how I cried. Late in the evening, Mom instructed me to call Mrs. Ann and tell her that I could not accept the job. I was absolutely devastated. With a trembling voice, I made what I thought was the phone call that would surely end my life and employment career. Most certainly, I was convinced that this call would surely end my aspirations for becoming gainfully employed. "After all", I thought to myself, "she promised to pay me $1.75 per week!" Gee, that was a lot of money. I pouted...in silence of course,...for what seemed like forever.

Mom and I did not talk about that incident until two years later. I'm convinced that she fully understood that racism existed, even in Farmhaven. She was simply not ready to discuss that issue and all of its ramifications. When we talked, she recounted that when she was nine years old, a white woman down the road in Farmhaven asked her father Papa Bozie, if one of his four daughters could come to their home on a weekly basis to clean and do other housekeeping chores. My grandfather did not allow my mom nor her sisters to do that. He wanted for his children a better way of life. For he too had experienced first-hand, the limited opportunities available for Blacks. A man of conviction and strong beliefs, he did not want this way of life for his daughters.

In the summer of 1954, I wanted to go to the "field" to chop and pick cotton. I had never been. All of my friends earned money throughout the summer by "going to the field" and doing other odd jobs. Finally, after begging all summer, in late August, Mom sat me down and explained that there was absolutely nothing wrong with working in the fields to earn a decent living. She wanted us to have the desire to earn money by working. However, as she explained, she held for her children a different set of beliefs, much like those of her parents. She too chose another way. There were some jobs that she did not want us to do. Not that she thought we were better than others, this is just her!

During this time, my father was earning only $18.00 per week and I thought I could do my part to help the family. Mom assured me that we would not go hungry nor cold and that most of our needs would be met. She explained that she had seen too many situations where individual's dreams and aspirations were stifled because they had gotten stuck in certain kinds of jobs. Her desire for us was to go to school to become educated and to get the kinds of jobs that would provide a better future for us. Both she and my dad as youngsters, picked cotton and worked in the fields for many hours each day.

She did not want us to experience some of the things that the two of them had been through. Again, she wanted a better way for her family.

In retrospect, after many years, I now understand clearly why I was not allowed to baby-sit or go to the field as a means of earning a living. Mom did not want us to get too comfortable, because she believed better opportunities were to come. The lesson was to reach higher. Most importantly, she did not want me in a position of vulnerability.

During the year I was twelve, Mom taught me to sew and allowed me to help her in her work as a professional seamstress. At the same time, I developed an interest in "fixin' hair." By the spring of 1955, I had a flourishing business. I charged $.75 for hair straightening and $1.25 for straightening and curling. By the time late Saturday evening rolled around, I would have made $12.00 - $15.00 for a week-end's work. Dad installed a gas jet in my room and I "fried curls" all week-end long. I was not allowed to wash hair in our home; so with freshly washed hair, the girlfriends came. I must confess, this proved to be better than baby-sitting for Mrs. Ann. By the time I was 13, my Dad took me "uptown" to open up my very own charge account at lupe's Department Store in our hometown.

These experiences did so much for me when I grew up and became a parent and homemaker. I remembered that parents appear to be old-fashioned and even a little strange to a thirteen year old. It was hard to believe they were ever teenagers or to believe they remembered the impact of their teen years. Now I know all too well that my parents were right. Their values remained constant and I am grateful.

Mom and Dad, I really love you. I thank you for all of the values you instilled in me. I love you more than words can say. In hindsight, they were always there for me, my brothers and my children, no matter what!!

My mom, (Mrs. Littie) and me, I was 15, she was...?

Mom and Dad in their "more seasoned" years.

Chapter 4

Childhood Years ~ Never Long Enough

The cliché that, "hindsight always gives one 20-20 vision", is all too true. My childhood was as normal as any childhood could be. Being raised by both parents, loved by two brothers and nurtured by loving relatives, provided the basis for me to gain strengths and values that I did not realize were being developed.

When my parents moved to Canton, we attended the Asbury United Methodist Church, located in our community. Immediately, the pastor's family, Rev. & Mrs. Thomas E. Davis, welcomed us as did the entire church family. Edgar Dean, their daughter, was about the same age as I. We became very close friends. We did all of the little girl things. The church was very active. There was singing, preaching, revivals and youth activities, all of which I enjoyed. It was also at that time that I was taking piano lessons at Holy Child Catholic School when I was asked to play for the youth choir at Asbury Church. Between my brothers, Edgar Dean's sisters, brother and several other children, we provided music for youth activities for the church.

One of the families that I still have warm and fond memories of in the church was the Carmichael's. Mother and Daddy Carmichael as they were affectionately called, took an active interest in my "plunking." Not only were they encouraging, but one Sunday, Mother Carmichael invited me to their home to visit so that I could play the piano for them. I was astonished to learn that Black folks had pianos in their homes. By society's standards, in those days, the Carmichael's were rich. Dean and I spent many Sunday's in their home. Mother Carmichael had a way of assuring us that the Sunday meal had been prepared especially for us and that we were their special guests. O, those baked Apples! She became for me, the grandmother I never knew. They were elderly, yet full of spunk. We spent hours singing the hymns. They told us Bible stories and were living examples of what Christianity represented.

To my utmost surprise, years after their deaths, their daughter-in-law, Aunt Berteil Carmichael wanted me to have their piano. It was a tremendous help to me because at that time, I had returned to Mississippi and was playing for various churches. Being able to practice any time I wanted to without having to go to a local church or to someone's home where there was a piano, was truly a blessing. Even today, the Carmichael's are still lovingly remembered by me and my family. As a matter of fact, many times Aunt Berteil and my mom are often mistaken for each other as they have many similarities.

Mr. & Mrs. George Carmichael, Sr.
(Mother and Daddy Carmichael)

About that same time, Dad was working for the Wright Appliance Store. He drove his employer's pick-up truck home each day from work and even kept it some week-ends. It was during that time that he taught Syd and me how to drive. Everyday, Syd and I met Dad at the comer from our house and he would let us take turns driving home sitting in his lap. The truck was an old stick shift and because of his patience, within a year, Syd and I had become "old stick-shift pros." Later in our teen-age years, dad bought an old car, a 1942 Chevrolet for $50.00 and gave it to Syd and me, with about fifty stipulations, of course.

Mom often reminds me how I used to boss my friends around. She lovingly recounts one incident in particular, *"The Dixon Store Story."* Mr. Dixon owned a neighborhood grocery store and every Saturday, after our chores were done, my girlfriends and I went to Dixon's store to treat ourselves and spend our allowances. One day, Mom recalls, Mr. Dixon complained that I was making my friends buy what I wanted them to buy, rather than what he wanted us to buy.

According to Mr. Dixon, I came in with a planned menu and told each friend what to purchase. I thought, since he sold a variety of cookies, chips and sodas, why not buy a variety so we could share as opposed to each of us buying the same kind of cookie, the same kind of chips and the same flavor of pop, as he suggested. My suggestion to them made perfect sense to me. Since we were regulars at his store, I could not understand his concern. As I grew older, I understood why he wanted us to buy the cookies he had selected, because they had been in the store, perhaps for many weeks. At mom's insistence, I stayed away from the store for a while until Mr. Dixon asked her to allow me and the friends to come back. In retrospect, we were probably his best customers. The story is still fun to tell. Mom has a way of embellishing it so it sounds better each time she tells it. <u>Childhood years are never long enough!</u>

One of the goals that our parents had was that of owning our own home. In 1954, their dream became a reality for them and we moved into our own brand new house. I had my very own room. Between the warm walls of this home, my individual characteristics continued to be developed. Our new home was in the community of the Mt. Zion Missionary Baptist Church, which was, and still is the largest Black Church in Canton. Immediately, I joined the church and became very active in many youth activities. I also played the piano and organ for Sunday School, the BTU, the Youth and Inspirational Choirs and for various church services, totaling more than 25 years.

Mother's goals for me were to learn to play the piano, to crochet and learn how to type. These were dreams that she had for herself as a young lady, but never had the opportunity to pursue. I took these goals to heart and achieved each one, just for my mom.

That same summer, five of us teen-aged girlfriends organized ourselves as the "CMUKLE'S", *(Crazy Mixed Up Kids Like Us)*. We went everywhere together. We went to the pool, to the movies, to church and to Tolliver's Cafe' on Saturday afternoons for ice cream. We were best friends. The CMUKLE'S were Alma, Mary, Bobby, Alba and me. We dressed alike and wore our hair alike; we were typical teenagers and remained long-time friends, even into our adult years.

I was thirteen when we re-enrolled in the Canton Public School District. That meant new friends and new situations. Mom had told me about the birds and the bees, so I kept one eye on the birds, the other eye on the bees. I was not allowed to "take company" until I was fourteen. Looking back, that sounds so young now. I could receive telephone calls and entertain at home every other week-end for two hours with close supervision, of course. Somehow the guys who called were afraid of my mom because she could give them the "fear of the Lord look"…, I knew that look all too well, so I couldn't blame them.

However, there was this one young man, a Preacher's Kid, (PK), who had a way with Mom. Even though she did not bend the rules very much, he was allowed to take me to the movies, to the prom and to other activities. He had a car, which was not necessarily a plus in Mom's eyes. Each time we went out, we were lectured about the rules and reminded to respect my parents' strict curfew. I really didn't mind; I expected them to stick to their rules. There were times I did not always agree with or understand all the rules. After becoming a parent, they all now make very good sense.

My teen-age years went so very fast. Between school activities, cheer-leading, being a drum majorette in the band, singing in the school choir, being very active in the church, spending time with my "girlfriends", doing chores at home, "fixin' hair", sewing, and helping to care for my younger brother, the years flew. They were good years, but were not long enough.

My high school sweetheart, the PK and I were married and moved to California where our two older children, Cynthia Verneatta and Edward, Jr., were born. We were proud parents. Our marriage ended in the early sixties and I returned home. We were both very young and clearly did not fully understand the inherent responsibilities of parenting.

Flonzie and Cynthia, our daughter, at age six months
Los Angeles, California, 1959

Chapter 5

A Tribute to My Children

One of my life's greatest challenges was to rear three children without the presence of their father. My youngest son, Lloyd Darrell, was born in Mississippi. He was named for my mom's baby brother who was killed tragically at age 3. The major focus was that at least for the next fifteen years, my life had to be put on hold so that my children could have every opportunity available to them. I learned many things during that time period, including, nothing takes the place of a father in the home. I would not trade one of my children, yet, if I had these years to repeat, I would make some changes. In trying to juggle a job or two, attend PTA and church meetings, school activities, shopping, sewing and all the many chores to keep the home going, I soon learned that my task would not be an easy one, but mom and dad were always there.

I thought it would be possible to design a formula to fit every conceivable situation. Because I was their mother, I thought everything would fall into place with my formula. I knew little about the individuality of each child. The concept of being mother and father sounded achievable. I began with a premise that my children were going to have everything that they needed and that they were not going to have to do without because their father wasn't present. Spending time with each one of them taught me many valuable lessons about parenting. Even so, I wasn't always sure that my decisions were right. There were many times I was afraid, but because I wanted to be a good mother, I had to trust my instincts and move forward. I spent a lot of time thinking about, the what if's? *"What if I let them down? What if I failed? What if, when they grew up, they wouldn't remember their home training?"* Finally, my resolve was to have faith that the time invested in their training would not be wasted. Since there was no training manual on parenting, therefore instincts had to be trusted. One's faith in God was essential in these situations.

My primary concern was to be the very best parent possible for my children. Canton still did not offer much in the way of jobs for Black females. In fact, my first job only paid $25.00 per-week. Were there a formula, it was my being resourceful to compensate for our lack of finances. One way was to teach and show my children love; the one thing money could not buy. I took the children to church instead of sending them. Each child was baptized at an early age: Cynthia as a Catholic, Ed and Lloyd Darrell as Baptists.

We spent time going to public places so they could learn how to interact and eat in public.

No matter how busy we were, we set aside time each month for the four of us to go out to a nice restaurant so that we could talk about things of interest to each of us. They took turns selecting our eating places, which gave them the opportunity to learn how to make choices. This also meant that I had to begin saving well in advance for the next month's outing. At this time, I was making $3,300.00 per-year working for an OEO funded poverty program, STAR, Inc. But, we made it!!

The children attended the Catholic School, as I had years before. It was important to me that the children receive a good quality education. Cynthia, the eldest child, assisted with chores and helped me take care of Ed and Darrell. She was an easy child to parent and was sensitive to my challenges of making ends meet. She loved singing and sewing.

Edward, Jr., was quite a character growing up. I had to watch him closely because he was fascinated with fire. He was a real little firebug. No matter what his punishment, he persisted in starting fires in the vacant field across from our apartment. He also loved tinkering around with lawn mowers and bicycles. In addition to cutting lawns, he soon became the neighborhood mechanic, while earning spending change.

Lloyd, the youngest, was quiet, a home-body and inquisitive. He questioned most things. He had to have reasonable answers as to why things were or were not a certain way. In his quiet unassuming way, he was and continues to be very caring and sensitive to the feelings of others. Even today, he remains inquisitive.

Throughout my years of mothering, my primary prayer for my children was two-fold; one was that the Lord would allow me to live long enough to see them become independent and self-sufficient. I did not want them to have to depend on anyone else for their survival. I wanted to do it. I was not and am not afraid of dying and I understood this was a selfish prayer, but God honored it. Second, I prayed daily, that my children would not be hurt or killed by fire. I remember when I was nine years old, as vividly as if it were yesterday, that a three-year-old child in our neighborhood had been burned to death. His mom had gone to town to purchase food for her children while they were still asleep. While she was away, the wood stove sparked and the house caught on fire. I can still see the undertaker coming in to get the little child who was burned beyond recognition. I have never forgotten that scene. As I became a mother, I kept those prayers constantly before the Lord. He honored each of those special prayer petitions, and many more. For His mercy, I am more than grateful.

By the time my children were teenagers, they each had a part-time job. I insisted that the jobs not interfere with their school requirements. It was necessary at times, to impose strict curfews for them.

I taught them the value of earning a decent living for themselves and not to be totally dependent on anyone as long as they were healthy and could work. During my single-parenting years, I was blessed to independently purchase two homes. It was very important to me that they have a home environment, one that provided them their own space, their own rooms, a yard, garden, a dog, kittens and even vacations. We lived in an apartment early on. It was never my intention nor desire to stay there long, not because it was not a nice place, but I desired something more comfortable for my children.

Each child was very different and developed his or her own mind-set as each grew and matured. They had certain ideas of their own that I had to reconcile. I respect each of them for their ability to think independently. Their contributions to my life are invaluable. My children taught me patience, they taught me how to respect and appreciate their individuality. When they spoke their opinions, I did not view them as being disrespectful. By the same token, they felt no inhibitions in expressing their love. Because I was eager to open my world to include them, accepting their views was not difficult for me. My children understood and respected the need for rules. They taught me within the rules however, there were areas for negotiations based on their own values and uniqueness's. We made the challenging times work.

Today, I stand proud with each of them and their accomplishments as they continue to pursue their dreams, hopes and aspirations. In their own way, they often show their appreciation for those years of nurturing. They have been and are good children. Even though everything has not been perfect, as nothing is, I am still proud to be their mom.

I learned many valuable lessons as a single parent. Much of what I experienced has been shared with many women who found themselves in similar situations. For the opportunity to share these experiences, I am most grateful. As I recount these experiences as a single parent, it can be rewarding and successful. Having a clear understanding that each child was and is a gift from God, has assisted me in accepting my status as a divorced mom. Our children must be protected. They deserve our best, so they can learn to give their best. If we do not assume this responsibility, then who will? How can we expect others to assist and encourage our children if we are unwilling to make those necessary sacrifices to ensure that they will be prepared to make good, sound decisions? It is our responsibility!

Let's just do it!

Cynthia, Ed and Lloyd ~ I Love You Dearly,

Ma…, 1979

(<u>Fast Forward</u>: Ed, lower left, passed away in 2014)

Part II

The Lord ~ The Shepherd of His People

A Psalm of David

The Lord is my shepherd;
I shall not want.
He maketh me to lie down in green pastures;
He leads me besides the still waters.
He restoreth my soul;
He leadeth me in the paths of righteousness
for His Name's sake,

Yea, though I walk through the valley of the shadow
of death,
I will fear no evil;
For thou art with me;
Thy rod and thy staff, they comfort me.

Thou preparest a table before me in the presence
of my enemies;
Thou anointest my head with oil;
My cup runneth over,

Surely goodness and mercy shall follow me
All the days of my life:
And I will dwell in the house of the Lord
Forever.

The 23rd Psalm; taken from
The Original African Heritage Study Bible
The King James Version

Chapter 1

Christian Values and Principles

Growing up as a young child in the church, I knew I wanted to be a Christian. While at that time I did not have a deep understanding of what that actually entailed, I was convinced that I wanted to be a Child of God. Being close to God offered a special kind of protection that I believed I needed. There was something so personal about the nurturance of my parents, my immediate and extended families, my neighbors and church members. I was touched by their sense of belonging to a God who could "do anything but fail." Having been taught Bible-based principles and values as a young child, there was something intriguing about these values that I wanted to be a part of my life.

When we lived in Farmhaven, we were within walking distance of The Old Truelight Baptist Church. My mom's home church, The Crossroads Church of God was also close to us. When we moved to Canton, we were in walking distance of the Asbury United Methodist Church, the Holy Child Jesus Church and the Mt. Zion Missionary Baptist Church. This allowed me to be consistently exposed to and involved in many church activities. In those years, denomination did not matter. We just went to church, sang, prayed, shouted and had a good time. What mattered most was being in church and in touch with the Master. We left church feeling as though we could make it yet another week no matter what our circumstances. We were anxious for the week to pass to return to fellowship once again with our church family. We knew that God was real. We were taught to depend on Him for our every need.

I learned that Jesus was and remains my friend. Knowing that I can come to Him, not only in times of adversity, but also in a spirit of praise and thanksgiving in those times when things are going well is so reassuring. To know there is nothing too hard for Him, that He accepts me at any point in my life, no matter how many mistakes I have made and no matter what happened, He still accepts me, "Just As I Am." God became a real force in my life as I played and sang the songs of Zion such as, "Pass Me Not, O Gentle Savior", "Jesus Keep me Near The Cross", "What a Friend We Have in Jesus", and other Songs of Faith.

I am amazed when I learned that my sins are thrown into the deepest part of the sea, never again to be remembered by Him. In spite of myself and of all the questionable things I do, God forgives me and continues to use me for His service. God opens doors and closes them in His own good time. As I think about how all these principles come together, I am overwhelmed. Christian values and principles were at work in our home, at play, in our school and in our community.

As a teenager, I learned that Jesus was my friend,
I have held to that belief, even to this day.

These were the years prior to the divisions between church and state. We began our school day, every day, with a prayer, the salute to the Flag and a song. Our school teacher might have also been our Sunday School Teacher, or our Baptist Training Union Leader, or our pastor's wife. All who served in those roles willingly shared their spiritual insights. We were eager to listen because of our respect for them and because we wanted to learn.

At a tender age, without fully realizing it, I was being molded for service, because I took these teachings to heart. As an adult, many of these instructions guided my thoughts and actions.

In the classroom, we spent time discussing Bible stories, exploring scriptures and singing church songs. Our teachers instructed us daily to be careful about our words and actions towards others. When we were unmindful, our punishment was to publicly apologize for our unacceptable behaviors. We may well have been embarrassed, but those experiences taught us to reflect on what we said about one another and how we treated each other in the future.

Many of these values came to mind when I became an adult. The principles I had been taught were used as bridge-builders in teaching my own children. I wanted them to learn what I had adapted as I watched these belief's being manifested through the lives of my parents, the elders and people in my own community.

Today we are overlooking a valuable resource in our communities. The wisdom of old age is unmatched. Young and old alike need to tap into the wisdom that the elderly bring to our society. I learned so much about the goodness and mercy of God from the church seniors who believed strongly in their principles. They exemplified their values through daily living. As youngsters, we may not have appreciated it then, but as the ol' folk use to say, *"chile', keep living, you will learn"*. Oh, how right they were. As a mom, those words are reassuring reminders that when you do what is right...for the right reason...the best is yet to come. I can truly say, I am a witness to their teachings because I learned from the best.

Chapter 2

The Lord is My Shepherd

As a child, I remember learning The Lord's Prayer, The Beatitudes, The 23rd Psalm and numerous other scriptures and verses from the Holy Bible. Learning the Bible and preparing for Sunday School at home, religious studies at the Holy Child Jesus School and studying on my own were all a part of my spiritual growth and development. It was not until later in life that I gained strength and a focused sense of value from these readings and activities.

Over the years, I have clung to the 23rd Psalm as though David wrote it especially for me. Every experience that I have had in my life can be found in some aspect of that Psalm. As I contemplate David sitting on the hillside watching the sheep and comparing his life to theirs, I can understand why he chose such beautiful language to describe the reassurance that only God can give.

He begins by saying, ***The Lord is MY Shepherd***. The opening sentence tells me that no matter what happens to me, I know that the Lord will not let me down. He will protect and take care of me. Regardless of the billions of people who occupy this world, He is their Shepherd too. *I shall not want.* I am assured that God will supply all of my needs. I may not have had everything that I thought I wanted, but all of my needs have been met. That's a promise He made to me as a young divorced mother of three children. I've never worried when times were lean and the pantry had little, I was always confident that my children were not going to go to bed hungry, and they haven't.

The *green pastures* represent times of harvest and prosperity. *Still waters* are peaceful. When I walk in the park or along a brook or a lake, I see the calmness and serenity of water. Water is cleansing; water is healing. When my mind is disturbed, walking "Down by the Riverside", helps me to experience a peace that passes all understanding. Nothing compares to that calm assurance.

There are times when *God restores my soul.* As I deal with broken fellowships, broken relationships and disappointments in my life, I am assured that there is healing and restoration. ***Fast Forward***: Over the years of chronicling my journey, I have lost both parents, both siblings, my eldest son Ed., Jr., and my husband, but..., but, I have never given up on God's promises. God leads *me in the paths of righteousness* so that His name will be glorified. Responding to His commission to stay on the path is one of my greatest joys as a Christian. This is not to say that I am perfect, because I am not, but I know who is, my Savior & Father.

Many times in my life, I have walked through valleys where *shadows of death* reside. There have been times when I have faced death as a Civil Rights Activist, only to be reassured that God did not give up on me. He was and is always there. I *need fear no evil* for He is with me and lets me know that His *rod and* His *staff* will always *comfort me.*

David's life is a clear example of man's ability to triumph over adversity. The power of choice lies within each of us. We often can create situations when we must choose what is good and what is not so good. In those times, it is important to be assured that when we have done our best and when negative situations occur, our focus must remain in-tact. Only God can assure and reassure based solely on our personal relationship with Him.

In today's world, just as in David's, good and evil exist. When we find ourselves in the presence of *enemies,* we can rise victorious. God's anointing provides us a hedge of protection, which remains when evil befalls. It's important for me to believe that *my cup runneth over* and that *goodness and mercy* do follow, all my days.

When this life is over, it's more than comforting to know that we will *live and dwell* in the house of the Lord forever. Most importantly, these promises are predicated upon a dedicated and committed life to God.

Having this reassurance in my life has given me the opportunity to thank God for being a Good Shepherd. I thank Him for allowing me to be a part of Him. For this reassurance, my hope is stayed.

Chapter 3

Molding Me For Service

In 1962, I returned to Canton from Los Angeles. As a young divorced mother, it was most difficult to adjust to and come to grips with the personal challenges that were before me. At such an early age, my real sense of mission and purpose had not been clearly defined. I believed that everyone had been created for a purpose, but I was not sure about my own. In some respects, I felt disadvantaged because of my new status as a young single mother with three small children. I was living back in my parents' home and we were dependent on them for our basic survival. Jobs in the South were almost non-existent for Black females. Those factors and more were overwhelming.

There were so many emotions I could not sort out The responsibilities of rearing three children were emotionally challenging. I had many doubts, many fears. My self-confidence was shaken. Although my sense of right and wrong was in-tact, I wasn't sure if I had the capacity to adequately teach them what they needed to know about real life situations. My questions were: "Can I really do this? Do I have the knowledge and information they need for their own growth and existence?" What would happen if they got into trouble?

For two years, I toiled with a multitude of emotions. I felt very vulnerable. I had to face countless uncertainties. That two-year period was the most important time of my life. I attended many private "pity parties" and experienced occasions of self-doubt. I carried around so much unnecessary baggage. It was during that same period, however, that God's assurance prevailed and I came to believe with certainty that even though I had a big responsibility, I could and would make it.

My faith in God was strengthened and restored as I went through those two years. It was a time of cleansing. It was a time of healing. Spending time getting to know myself was one of the most valuable experiences that I have had. I developed a sense of my abilities, my limitations and my potential. I learned who I was. I am not **"all that"**, just confident!

The values that I learned early in my life enhanced my ability to redirect my focus. I knew I had to get on with the business of fulfilling my assignment. I learned the distinct difference between a job and an assignment. A job is from 9 to 5 while an assignment is the work of a lifetime, 24/7. While many uncertainties still remained, I was able to forge ahead with a clearer sense of my mission and purpose. The challenges were faced head-on, with clarity and much prayer, then and now.

At the end of this two-year ordeal, I evolved as a person who was confident that God had commissioned me to be a special messenger. My decision to become involved in the struggle for mankind was not an easy one. I believed for sure that was what God wanted me to do.

It took some time for me to accept this mission. I spent time in denial. I spent time running from my mission and procrastinating. I spent time wondering what people would think. I spent time making excuses and asking, "Why me?"

I debated with God. I said, "Lord, you know I stutter when I get excited, I have a speech impediment, you know I get nervous when speaking before crowds. Why would you want me in a role of leadership when I don't speak well?" (I am really a behind-the-scenes person).

Then He reminded me of Moses who also had a speech impediment. With His calm assurance, He said to me, "Share with others what I have given you and I will speak for you. Lo, I am with you always, even until the end of the world; and as I provided for the Prophets of old, I will provide for you". I can say with certainty, He has! Even today, I still get nervous on a public stage, I've learned how to better manage it.

I used another excuse. I said, "Lord, I'm not famous." Nobody knows me, God reminded me that you did not chose the Civil Rights Movement, it chose you.

"Lord, I have no money, no job and three children." He reminded me saying, "I own everything, and *while you will never be rich, you will always have what you need.* I will never leave you nor forsake you."

"Lord," I argued, "believe it or not, I really am very shy."

His response was, "I made you in my image and likeness. I will prepare you to take this message to those who need to hear it." I will speak for and through you. **I've Got Your Back!!**

In all my endeavors, I have tried not to lose sight of the
promises that we made, God and I.
With clear instructions, my admonition was:

"Go! Go! Go!
There are people who are hurting.
There are children who are sick.
There are elderly who need you.

Go!
There are people who need a sense of value.
There are young mothers who need a listening ear.
There are people who have faced discrimination in all forms.

Go!
There are people who need job training.
There are people who need to have their minds liberated.
There are people who need encouragement to register and vote.

Go!
You've got to Go!
I Am Molding You For Service.
You've got to Go!
I am preparing you to take a message to a hurting world.
GO! GO! GO!"

The opportunities have been unimaginable!!

1988~Washington, DC

Introduction to Part III
Civil Rights

I felt apprehensive in preparing to chronicle the events which occurred while I was actively involved in the civil rights struggle. It was important to analyze fully the reasons for these feelings of apprehension. I tried to have a clear vision of what was at the heart of these emotions. In my mind, I have been writing this book for at least twenty years. There have been many times when I've begun to pen these experiences only to find that my emotions were much too overwhelming. Again, I knew I was not ready. There were inner feelings that I could not understand or admit to. Feelings on one hand which prompted the thought, "Why now?" Other thoughts said, "Not yet". I followed those latter emotions until I became convinced that the time had come. I know now beyond a doubt, 1994 was the time!

My personal reflections as well as a vast array of memories of my experiences during the civil rights years are played out in vivid detail. I can see the national guards with their rifles, I can resurrect my feelings of being tear gassed, going to jail, being shot at, having my life threatened as well as the lives of my children, I simply was not ready to deal with my pain. Only when I accepted the reality of these experiences in my life, could I move ahead with intensity, enthusiasm and energy.

As an individual, it is difficult for me to admit pain in my life. More than that, as I struggled with my memories, it was most difficult to deal with the genesis of pain. Most of all, it was not always easy to reconcile the results of pain. I often thought I might have failed in a particular area of my life. There were other times when I felt I could have or should have done something differently. Only after acknowledging that I was hurting could I openly and quickly deal with the source of the pain and its symptoms. This was yet another valuable learning experience for me. Validating the pain and hurt in my life was crucial to my ability to deal with the pain as opposed to continuing to push it back into the recesses of my mind.

As with all emotions, pain manifests itself in many ways. Sometimes during this period in my life, it was manifested in ways in which I had little or no control. This writing experience has allowed me to reconcile, work through and put to rest once and for all, my personal struggle with anger and pain.

Chapter 1
The Pain Struggle

In the early 1960's, while living in Los Angeles, and adjusting to my role as a new wife and new mother, the civil rights movement exploded into my awareness. I watched in disbelief as the public drama of this movement unfolded. Frankly, I knew very little about this whole civil rights business. That may sound strange for someone who was born in Mississippi and grew up in a place where segregation was a way of life.

My lack of understanding can be attributed to several factors: I grew up in a home where racism was not talked about. We were taught emphatically to believe in ourselves. Our parents fostered in us a belief that we could become whomever or whatever we wanted to become. They demonstrated their beliefs by their willingness to teach us at home, to spend quality time with us and to provide for our needs through their hard work. They used all of their creative energies to thereby ensure our achievements even though they knew all too well the realities of their own daily encounters with segregation---Mississippi style.

Additionally, the nuns who taught us during our years at Holy Child Jesus Catholic School were also all white. This fact did not seem at all unusual to my brothers and me. After all, they were committed to equality and encouraged us to achieve through hard work. Actually, they were validating the teachings and expectations of our parents.

My mom's family is closely related to whites in Canton/Madison and Leake Counties. During our years in Farmhaven, we lived among relatives, both black and white. We all visited back and forth from time to time. None of these situations openly exposed me to racism or segregation. The closest we came to questioning institutionalized racism as children was rooted in our observations of the faces of white children were being bussed to their segregated schools while we walked to ours. It was later in life that I understood more clearly the systemic racism that was evident in the educational system.

Watching the daily news while living in Los Angeles, I was glued to the television set as I looked at the scenes of racial unrest as they unfolded. There were sit-ins and voter registration marches. People were being sprayed with pressurized water hoses. They were being beaten, trampled to the ground by horses, being jailed and even killed.

The Freedom Rides were in full swing in 1961. When I saw the burning of the bus in Alabama by Klansmen, I was beyond being horrified.

Each day the news was replete with these scenes, many of them in my home state, some of them in my hometown. I saw scores of people, Blacks and whites, most of them young, who were brought into Mississippi and other southern states to participate in integrating the beaches, public accommodation facilities and the lunch counters.

The volunteers marched hand-in-hand and arm-in-arm with Black citizens, they attended mass meetings and rallies and accompanied them to their local registrar's office to attempt voter registration. These televised images ignited an inner struggle. I remembered the safety and security of my years growing up in the South. These scenes conflicted greatly with my memories and produced an intense sense of frustration, anger, humiliation and personal pain.

I often talked with my parents who shared with me their personal accounts of events that were occurring in Canton and their explanations of the reasons for the unrest. Their sense of disbelief was similar to mine. They could not believe that some white persons with whom they had passed the time of day, persons with whom they had worked, persons with whom they had conducted business transactions—all of a sudden transformed themselves into violent strangers. Relatives, co-workers, strangers and friends, were being beaten, maimed and jailed. Mom and Dad still tried to protect me from the harsh realities of their daily experiences. I then remembered and understood quite vividly, why I could not babysit for Mrs. Ann.

My children and I returned to Mississippi in the late Spring of 1962. Canton was a **hot spot!** There were mass meetings every night, daily and hourly strategy sessions, an active selective buying campaign, sit-ins and marches. Local, state and national television and newspaper reporters and local citizens filled the streets. The atmosphere was one of strange excitement and busy-ness. The Black community was flooded with leaflets from <u>The Madison County Citizen</u> and other community bulletins which kept the Black community abreast of current events. There was so much going on, it was hard to keep up with all the activities. So many citizens of Canton put their lives on the line daily because they believed what they were doing was right.

As I more clearly understood the effects of institutionalized racism, I realized it was people like Mr. Harry Archie, Mr. Rosemore Boyd, Mr. & Mrs. W. E. Garrett, Both Mr. & Mrs. C. O. Chinn, Sr., and Junior, members of their families, Mrs. Annie Devine, Mr. Wilbur Robinson, Mr. George Raymond, Rev. Bennie Luckett, Father Like Mikschl, Rev. P. F. Parker, Judge U. S. Rimmer, Rev. James McRee and scores of others who set the standards of courage for those of us who later became involved.

Special recognition is due to Mr. and Mrs. George Washington, Sr., who allowed one of their properties known as the "Freedom House" to shelter many of the civil rights workers, especially those from the North, and would not have easily found local housing. Their bravery and dedication are to be commended. In spite of threats and acts of violence against them, they stood firmly in the face of personal injury and potential loss of life and income.

Many individuals who were involved at that time, have passed on. People from every locale, who represented all races, ethnicities and cultures contributed unselfishly "to the cause" for those who had little or no hope. It is important to acknowledge and recognize their contributions.

An Historical Church of Refuge

Mt. Zion Missionary Baptist Church was one of the very few churches which opened their doors to the civil rights movement in Canton. I am proud to have been a member of this church from age 12 in 1954 until I moved away in 1989. The church is now pastored by Dr. W. L. Johnson, Sr., who is much like Rev. P. F. Parker. Dr. Johnson also strives to improve community relations and to build strong families through God's word. It pleases me to be able to say that his gracious wife, First Lady Lena and I, were classmates and have remained dear friends.

Mt. Zion served as a refuge for many. A number of those individuals involved in the struggle were and are members of this great church.

The Mt. Zion Missionary Baptist Church ~ Canton, Mississippi
Rev. P. F. Parker, Pastor ~ 1964
For more than 40 years, Mt. Zion has been pastored
by Dr. W. L. Johnson, Sr.

A reprint from the Madison County Citizen
April 20, 1964

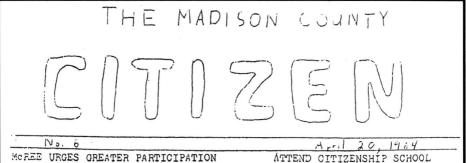

THE MADISON COUNTY CITIZEN

No. 6   April 20, 1964

McREE URGES GREATER PARTICIPATION

Today we are in the midst of a struggle for the dignity of man. Never before in the history of this great country has so much been said about a problem facing us and yet so little accomplished. We have heard it said time after time that this is only a racial problem. It is more than a racial problem, it is a human problem that affects all freedom loving people.

We have been accused of a number of things, but one thing we have never been accused of and that is seeking freedom. Our city, county, and state have made a mockery of Constitutional government, crying for state rights and not human rights. We are having these mass meetings in order for you to be informed about the truth.

You read the daily press and you only get the view that the local power structure wants you to have. In a court order it was said that there had been no effort on the part of the Negro community to discuss these problems. We mailed two letters to local officials and received no reply.

We have Negro teachers in our public schools who have finished our so-called equal state colleges and some have MA degrees. Yet, they cannot vote. Why? We are asking you to come to St. Paul AME Zion Church on Monday night at 7:00Pm and let the power structure know you are dissatis- fied and you are not going to move away but stay here and fight for human dignity.

Rev. J.F. McRee

ATTEND CITIZENSHIP SCHOOL

On Sunday, March 22, 1964 at 5:30 P M, Mrs. Rosa Clay and Mrs. Marian Robinson departed from Jackson, Mississippi for the Dorcester Center in McIntosh, Georgia, for a week in Citizen- ship school training. The basic teaching of the school dealt with literacy. Citizenship schools enable the students to pass literacy tests for voting and teach how to read and write. They also teach about general community problems such as recreation, health, and improved home life. Citizenship schools provide badly needed education. They are open to all people who have problems related to first class citizenship and want to do something about them.

After a week of intensive training, we departed for home, where we then set up our own classes. We need more people interested to be trained for Citizenship School teachers. If you're interested in teaching, contact the COFO office at 838 Lutz Avenue for more information. Mrs. Rosa Clay and Mrs. Marian Robinson.

POLITICAL EDUCATION AT APRIL MEETING

Next Sunday the Council of Federated organizations will hold its monthly meeting at the Masonic hall on Lynch Street in Jackson. The meeting will be a workshop aimed at helping everyone understand the political structures of Mississippi. All Madison County people are urged to attend. The conference will start at 11:00 AM.

ALL GOOD CITIZENS SHOULD KNOW THESE WORDS

Negroes all over the state are studying to learn about the political structure of their state. They are learning who chooses candidates. They are learning how all people should participate in a democracy. It is important to understand the words on this page. Study this page carefully and save it to look at when you forget something.

PRECINCT or WARD

A precinct and ward are the same thing. All people who live in the same precinct vote in the same place. All the people who live in the West Ward in Canton voted at the Veterans Home in the last state election.

A man finds out what ward or precinct he is in when he becomes a registered voter or by asking someone who lives near him who knows. All the people in a precinct live in the same area. For example, all the people who live west of Union Street in the Canton area are in the West Ward (or precinct).

BEAT or SUPERVISOR'S DISTRICT

A beat and a supervisor's district are the same thing. There are five beats in Madison County. Each beat is divided into precincts or wards. For example, the first beat (where Canton is) is divided into the North Ward, the South Ward, and the West ward.

One of the duties of a good citizen is to know what Beat and precinct he lives in. If you live near Canton, you live in Beat one. If you live near Flora, you live in Beat two. If you live near Madison you live in Beat Three. If you live near Sharon or Farmhaven in the eastern part of the county you live in Beat Four. If you live in the North part of the County, near Camden, you live in Beat Five.

CONGRESSIONAL DISTRICT

A Congressional District is not the same as a Supervisor's District. A Congressional District is much larger. Each Congressional District has many counties inside of it. We live in the Fourth Congressional District. Some of the cities in our district are Canton, Carthage, and Meridian.

All of the people in a Congressional District have the same representative in Congress. That is why it is called a Congressional District. One of the jobs of that representative is to look out for needs of the people in his district.

ALL GOOD CITIZENS SHOULD KNOW THESE WORDS

Chapter 2

Caught Up

Canton became a melting pot where all major organizations established their presence. There was The Council of Federated Organizations (COFO), The Congress of Racial Equality (CORE), The National Association for the Advancement of Colored People (NAACP), The National Council of Churches (TNCC), The Mississippi Freedom Democratic Party (MFDP), Voter Education Project (VEP), The Student Nonviolent Coordinating Committee (SNCC), The Madison County Movement (MCM), The Madison County Union for Progress (MCUP), The Southern Christian Leadership Conference (SCLC), and others. The main focus of each was the liberation of Blacks, at that time referred to as "Coloreds or Negroes". Canton and Madison County were chosen for this high energy activity because of the high concentration of Blacks. Nearly 30,000 people lived in Madison County. Almost seventy-percent of the residents were Black. At that time, however, just over one hundred Blacks in the entire county were actually registered to vote.

In the Spring of 1963, my children and I went to Biloxi to spend time with my cousin, Ethel. There, like many towns in the deep South, where everyone's mind was "Stayed on Freedom." On the streets, in the supermarkets, in the department stores, in the churches, in the schools, local Black businesses and everywhere there was talk about freedom.

I had found employment in the center of the Black community in a little restaurant. Every day three Black attorneys from the NAACP came in to eat and talk about what was going on. It was during this time, the spring and summer of 1963, that attempts were made to integrate the beaches on the Gulf Coast. National guardsmen had been called, state policemen had been summoned to serve as back up to local law enforcement officials. The attorneys talked about who had been beaten, who they had to get out of jail and what to expect when the beaches were actually integrated. I received much of my "freedom education" from them. They were the best teachers, after all, they were the three Black Mississippi Attorneys: R. Jess Brown, Jack Young, Sr., and Carsey Hall. These astute civil rights attorneys represented many disenfranchised Blacks during those turbulent days. As my interest heightened, I couldn't wait for them to come in every day for my "history lesson." They didn't realize until much later that they provided me direct instruction in the legal aspects of the freedom movement. The local branch of the NAACP was very active on the coast (Biloxi, Gulfport, Pass Christian, and Pascagoula). On one of their visits to the restaurant, Attorney Young asked me attend a night rally. I agreed and joined in participating in integrating the beaches in Biloxi in 1963.

There were more mass meetings, more voter registration activities, more rallies, more public demonstrations, more boycotts, more sit-ins, more marches to the County Court-house, beatings and all that one can imagine, and some things you can't.

Medgar Evers was assassinated on June 12, 1963. He was Field Secretary for the Mississippi State Conference of Branches for the NAACP. The news about his death was traumatic to me and thoughts about his murder absolutely seared my heart. I knew then I had to become involved in this great movement. At that point, the extent of my commitment to the cause was still undetermined.

As the news of Medgar's death became public, more national guardsmen and state troopers were called in. The streets filled quickly with townspeople who began demonstrating, singing freedom songs, marching, being arrested and basically defying the directions from the law enforcement officials. Adding to this frenzy of noise were sounds of sirens, ambulances and bullhorns.

I reported to work at the restaurant that evening as usual, but because of the unrest, the owner announced that all of the Black businesses were closing and all employees had to be escorted home. Violence was anticipated and it did occur. As demonstrators attempted to integrate the beaches along the Gulf Coast, there were beatings, shootings, arrests, jailing's, fire bombings and almost everything imaginable.

As events following the assassination of Medgar unfolded, it made me sick to my soul. If, because of his beliefs, a man could be gunned down in the yard of his home, in the presence of his wife and children, then what could I do? Sadly, his wife, Myrlie, had suddenly become a widow and a single parent. She would have to be both mother and father to her children, a pain I knew all too well. I silently wondered how she was going to explain to her little children that their father died because of racial hatred and bigotry. Everything I had been taught to believe in was now being challenged by this senseless act. The question that haunted me was: "How could this happen in America?" The foundations of my basic beliefs in the concepts of freedom and equality were absolutely being ripped apart. I recalled many other heinous murders.

If Medgar Evers gave his life for this cause, then certainly there was something I had to do. I did not sleep for several nights, not because of any fear of personal loss of life, but because of my agonizing decision to become involved. I felt I had a lot to lose, especially my three small children. I had been taught to step out on faith when I felt I was right. I remained in Biloxi until early fall and became involved in activities there. I then returned to Canton, energized and ready to work.

I began to understand more clearly Medgar's message: *"The body may be killed, but the vision will **not** die."* My time to become involved had come. Even though I did not know him, his death brought me into his world as real as a friend or relative. It was my wake-up call and a defining moment.

Every town had its own uniqueness and its own special place in the movement. Canton was no different. Canton's special uniqueness was played out in a number of combative measures used by the "establishment" to keep Blacks...so called…, in their place.

Voter registration was at the heart of our collective struggle. We finally realized the path to our freedom was through the ballot box. The establishment believed just as strongly that the key to maintenance of the status quo was in their continued denial of our access to the vote.

The most powerful representative of the establishment was the local registrar. Throughout the South, these individuals were most creative in denying Black citizens the right to register and to vote. In Madison County, as well as in other Mississippi counties, the local registrar used various forms of intimidation, reprisal, threats, harassment and retaliation to maintain their power. This was accomplished in many ways. Voter suppression was alive and well in the Deep-south.

There was a big push by Blacks to become registered voters. The "establishment", through the local registrar, was just as determined to deny Blacks that constitutionally guaranteed right. The Mississippi poll tax provided local registrars with a means to practice legalized discrimination. It required evidence of land ownership prior to an individual's registering to vote. Potential Black voters had to actually show their annual poll tax receipt to the Registrar prior to registration. Not many Blacks in the city owned land; thus, they were not allowed to register nor to vote. Many of those who owned land in the County were afraid to attempt to register for fear of reprisal.

Local white Priest, Fr. Luke Mikschl, was a strong advocate for Blacks

Retaliation and reprisal came in various forms. When Blacks would come to register, without fail, the Registrar provided their names to the local newspaper. Whether they were allowed to register or not, many lost their jobs. The purpose of publishing their names was to identify them as potential "trouble makers" and to alert their local white employers for purposes of possible termination. The resulting fear and intimidation prompted many to delay returning to register for long periods of time.

One hurdle Blacks faced when they went to register was the 21-item two-page Registration Questionnaire. The questionnaire for white voters contained only six questions. Black voters also had to interpret a section of the Mississippi Constitution to the Registrar's satisfaction. Sections of the constitution were cut into small folded slivers and placed in a cigar box. At item number 17, prospective voters had to pull out a section at random and write their interpretation on the questionnaire. He could deny access to registrants as many times as he wanted. According to Mississippi law, the prospective voter **could not** return until another 30 days had passed. Many times potential Black voters became so discouraged and frustrated they would choose not to return at all. This was the registrars' intent.

To be considered qualified, a Black voter would have already met the requirements as set by the Registrar. A most insidious tactic used by the Registrar to keep Blacks from voting was the writing of a variety of phrases or words next to or over the names of qualified voters. In some cases, these persons would have already voted in other prior elections.

Often when persons arrived to vote, to their dismay, they discovered their names had been scratched out and the words "moved to another precinct", "moved to another state", "disqualified", or even the word "deceased" had instead been written in many instances. Consequently, those legally registered voters would have to vote a challenged ballot. There was no guarantee that it would be counted. It was left to the Registrar's discretion, who was spokesman for the Madison County Board of Election Commissioers.

The challenged ballot was a separate voting procedure which required voters to present proof of their viability. They had to prove they were living beings. Acceptable forms of proof were driver's license, a marriage license, a birth certificate, or a social security card. It might have even been a property deed. Once the required documents were produced, the voter then had to vote on a separate paper ballot, place that ballot in a separate box and leave the area knowing that all the ballots in the box were supposed to be counted separately, or maybe not at all. Voters required to go to a different precinct expected to suffer the same indignities. Upon arrival, in many instances, they still had to vote a challenged ballot. By design, the challenged ballots were counted by an "all white" Board of Election Commissioners. One can only surmise what happened to those ballots. Even today, we question whether or not those ballots were really actually all counted. Probably **NOT!**

When I went to register, I purposely went alone as I knew violence could happen. I was given the two page questionnaire. When I got to item no.17, I went to the cigar box and pulled out the section of the Constitution on "habeas corpus." I didn't know what it meant and I'm convinced that the Registrar did not either. I completed the questionnaire and proceeded to write my response to the Constitution question. When I finished, he reviewed my answer and told me I did not pass. I asked him to explain my error. <u>He responded in a harsh tone stating,</u> *"**Nigger, I told you, you did not pass, now get the hell out of my office!**"* Even if the Registrar was having a "good day," the extent of one's preparation did not matter; his word was law. I felt a sickening frustration and questioned how one person could wield so much "home-made" power over another. It angered me to know that one person could determine when or how I could exercise my rights under the Constitution. As I walked down to corridor of the county courthouse, I became more determined to answer the call to run for office. A number of residents continuously asked me to run for office, but because I doubted myself...until that day..., I had refused. That day, I said to myself, **"I'm gonna run for office and I'm gonna get your job!**

It was the law that when one failed the literacy test, they could not return for 30 days. Determined to pass the next time, I used the next 30 days to study the entire Constitution. When I returned, I pulled out the same section as before: "habeas corpus". This time after he reviewed my response, he told me I passed and allowed me to write my name in the registration book. I felt great pride as I walked out of his office and down the halls of the Madison County Court House. I was now considered a *first class citizen.* As I left the Court House, I could not help but wonder, however, if there were any other sections in the box besides that of "habeas corpus."

That single event convinced me that the time would come when I must make a difference. In the months and years to come, I would have the opportunity to teach voter registration classes. I would be privileged and honored to register Black voters in the same Historic Madison County Court House, a symbol of injustice..

In Madison County, Blacks represented the majority of the potential voting population, yet no Blacks held any county-wide elected offices. As we began to organize our efforts, it was clear that we had two very important tasks. We had to convince Black citizens to register. Then we had to convince our fellow citizens of the importance of exercising their right to vote. Fear was very real in the Black community. There were a few courageous Blacks who were willing to seek public office. We were reminded continually that the Registrar was very arbitrary in exercising his options of disqualifying registered voters and refusing to certify the candidates' petitions. It was that same registrar who had to certify that persons who signed the qualifying petition for a candidate, were also bonafide registered voters. Blacks had a difficult time becoming qualified candidates. Even if we presented a challenge, in many instances and by design, the election could well be over by the time a court decision was rendered.

There were daily marches to the Registrar's office by local Blacks who wanted to register. Their courage was amazing. It was their willingness to risk intimidation and retaliation that inspired others to "keep on keeping on". Many were afraid, but we kept on prayin', we kept on walkin', we kept on singin' and we kept on marchin' up to freedom land..., the Court House. Some of the churches played a major role in encouraging parishioners to be involved, thus validating that civil rights was a just cause, as espoused by Dr. Martin Luther King, Jr., as well as many local residents.

Rev. Simon Johnson and local residents marching to the Madison County Courthouse to register to vote in 1964 in Canton, Mississippi

I cannot say when my involvement actually began. I remember waking up one morning being *caught up* in that civil rights "mess" as it was commonly referred to by townspeople. It was as if I were being driven by a force outside of myself. I had to do my part for freedom. The more things happened, the more I knew that I had to stand up for what I felt was right. I felt a great sense of responsibility to make myself available to help in this struggle. I was *caught up* in a certain time and place in history. I was *caught up* in a cause that held many uncertainties. I was *caught up* in what would hold many problematic situations. Most of all, I was *caught up* without a choice. Witnessing this cruel beating, strengthened my resolve to continue.

A local resident being man-handled and beaten by local white policemen.

This scene was repeated all too often as Black citizens gathered to register. Many were beaten, jailed, thrown in cattle cars, trucks and police wagons. These acts of reprisal only strengthened our resolve to become first-class citizens. I was in the crowd and personally witnessed this beating.

Each time citizens were subjected to this type of inhumane and violent treatment, larger groups of local citizens would become involved. The driving force in our minds was that we could not all be beaten, we could not all be jailed. We were prepared to do what was necessary to complete the journey we had begun. Many people, both local and out-of-state, were brutally maimed. It became clearer and clearer that changing these types of violent acts towards Blacks was going to be a long process, but we were determined and we would not retreat. It was the singing of Freedom Songs that encouraged us that "We Shall Not Be Moved, A'int gonna let **NOBODY** turn me 'round, turn me 'round, turn me 'round, I'm gonna keep on walkin', keep on talkin', marchin' up to freedom land." Our songs made us free.

Chapter 3

Getting My Feet Wet

Almost every night there were mass meetings: "freedom meetings" as they were called. Most of the meetings were held in the Pleasant Green Church of Christ Holiness, USA. At first, many of the local churches would not allow these meetings to be held in their sanctuaries. It took a while for some of the Black ministers to understand that the movement was not just a social issue. It was a moral issue, an issue of conscience, more importantly, it was an issue of Christianity. Many of the rural churches in Madison County did not have this concern. Ironically, many of the churches in the county readily opened their doors for us to meet, to organize, to pray and to sing.

Beginning in the Fall of 1963, there was an all out effort to bring the Head Start Program to Canton. The Child Development Group of Mississippi (CDGM). This was a group of parents and community people dedicated to the cause of education and was housed at Mt. Beulah, an abandoned small residential education center. This center was located in rural Edwards, Mississippi. Our goal was to create a system in the State of Mississippi, which would provide pre-school education for our children. In addition to housing the state-wide Head Start Program, Mt. Beulah became a site for training seminars and other kinds of civil rights activities. Scores of us involved in these efforts were trained by Marian Wright, now Edelman.

We went back and forth to Mt. Beulah. Few of us had jobs or other resources. We had no funds. We borrowed cars. We car-pooled. We caught rides. We borrowed gas money and engaged in as many creative activities as possible to ensure our message was heard. Our central focus was providing better opportunities for our children that we did not have.

In the training seminars, we learned how to write and submit proposals for funding. This was the first time many of us had been involved in these kinds of collective initiatives. Our minds began to come alive as we thought about the kinds of services we wanted to provide for our children. At first, because of limited funding, we were unable to implement all facets of our proposals. When the funds were received, we faced another challenge. We had great difficulty in convincing many local congregations in Canton and Madison County to use their facilities to house Head Start.

Mrs. Clarice Dillon Coney, was responsible in great part, for Canton's involvement in the OEO federally funded Head-start program. Fearless in her commitment to the Mt. Beulah Project, she was an inspiration to hundreds of activists, both county and state wide.

Mrs. Coney became State Education
Director for the Mississippi Head Start
Program.

Many churches where Head Start and the Freedom Schools were housed were often bombed, burned and vandalized. There were a series of attempts to scare us and force us to retreat from our beliefs. Mt. Beulah continued to be our primary planning and training site along with Tougaloo College. From Mt. Beulah, which was private property, there was a lonely five to seven mile stretch of road leading to the main highway taking us back to our homes. Some of us lived in Jackson, the rest lived in Canton. There was always the threat of violence. We never knew what form it would take. Local gun-totin' whites who opposed any form of unity and progress for Black folks would lie in wait as a show of force and intimidation. Rationality seemed to leave them as we began to assert ourselves. As the importance of voter registration and other forms of empowerment became a reality for us, hatred and fear began to over-take the white establishment.

We became easy prey for vicious acts of violence. Men and women were pulled from their cars and beaten. Cars became moving targets as their tires and windows were shot out. On any given night, we faced truck loads of men intent on frightening, maiming or even killing us.

Community people were always warned to leave Mt. Beulah before dark and to be on the main highway by dusk. On one of our training trips, Mrs. Coney and I (just the two of us as we often did) had driven to Mt. Beulah for training. On this particular day, the training was a bit longer than usual. By the time we left, it was getting dark and a truck filled with Klansmen followed us as I was driving, The driver bumped my car several times and ran us off the road. Dad had taught me to drive a stick-shift when I was a young child and when I was finally able to gain control of my vehicle, I steered it back on the road. It was then that someone in the truck shot at us, endangering our lives even more. By the grace of God, I maintained controlled of the car as we were just at the main highway. The truck turned around and we were safe. Mrs. Coney and I often talk about that near death experience. We were in grave danger and we knew all to well the stories of so many others who had "gone-out just like that!"

As buildings were being bombed and destroyed by fire, it was remarkable how quickly Blacks managed to rebuild those facilities. It was as if we had "caught a fever" and nothing could stop our determination. It seemed as if the more the acts of violence increased, the more Blacks united around the cause. It was very evident that we clearly believed that our cause was right. The challenge was to do or die. We understood the possibility of dying was the price we were willing to pay for our beliefs.

CORE's Building Bombed

St. Paul Dispatch 6/5/64

CANTON. MISS. — (AP) — A civil rights organization's headquarters here was shaken today by a predawn blast apparently caused by an explosive hurled against the building.

No one was injured and only minor damage was reported. Landy McNair, one of two Congress of Racial Equality workers inside the building at the time, said the explosive bounced off the front wall and exploded in the sidewalk.

This was the second incident in three weeks at the building — called the Freedom house by CORE workers. In the earlier incident, three shots were fired into the building. No one was hurt.

CORE workers have been pushing a Negro voter registration drive in this central Mississippi town about 30 miles north of Jackson for several months.

Thursday, September 17, 1964
The St. Paul Dispatch

Fire Destroys Freedom School

CANTON, MISS. —(UPI)— A Negro church used recently as a voter registration school was destroyed by fire early today.

Authorities confirmed that the St. John's Baptist church near the rural community of Valley View went up in flames shortly after midnight.

The FBI in Jackson said it was investigating.

Negro leaders said two white men were seen at the church, located in a rural area, about five minutes before the fire broke out. They said they had identities of the two men and would turn the information over to federal authorities.

The St. John's church was used as a freedom school by integration workers during the summer months and had been a headquarters for voter registration work among Madison county's Negro population.

Madison County Sheriff Jack Cauthen said he was investigating the incident. He said this was the second Negro church in the county to be burned this summer.

It makes the 23d Negro house of worship in Mississippi to be either damaged or destroyed by fires of mysterious origin since Negro leaders stepped up desegregation activities in the state at the beginning of the summer.

The entrenched priority on the agenda for all the civil rights organizations in Canton, in Madison County and throughout the South was voter registration. This issue was at the heart of all activity. In our attempts to register, marches to the court house occurred regularly. On many occasions, Blacks were turned away by local law officials. We were arrested, jailed and beaten as we continued our quest for equality through the voter registration process. We knew we could change things if only we could get the right to vote. We were not going to give up until we obtained that right.

Blacks being surrounded by law enforcement officers and being forced to retreat for attempting to march to the Madison County Courthouse in 1964

In November of 1963, Black citizens across the state organized a "mock" election. This effort had two major purposes: 1). This unofficial election would determine our voting strength; and, 2). It would also dispel the myth that Blacks **would** vote if given the opportunity. Despite constitutional guarantees and earlier laws which ensured the rights of all citizens, Blacks still could not register and vote without fear of intimidation and reprisal. The mock election, called the *Freedom Vote,* was an overwhelming success. Approximately 80,000 Blacks turned out in record numbers across the state thereby demonstrating and affirming the potential of our voting power.

Our candidates were African American Dr. Aaron Henry and Rev. Edwin King, who was Caucasian. Dr. Henry, candidate for Governor and the State President of the NAACP, opposed two powerful white political figures, Paul B. Johnson and Rubel Phillips. Rev. King, a white civil rights worker and long time supporter of humanitarian causes, opposed Carrol Gartin and Stanford Morse for the office of Lieutenant Governor. On "mock election day", even though our candidates were the undisputed winners, officially, and sad to say, this election did not count, because our right to become qualified voters, by law, had not been completely secured. Rev. King, Chaplain at Tougaloo College, still wears facial scars from a severe beating he received for being a supporter of and advocate for our cause.

There were many whites who also suffered all types of violence, including loss of life. I salute those white sisters and brothers who clearly understood this cause and were willing, if necessary, to even sacrifice their lives. As a result of this mock election, we knew that: *Hands that picked cotton could now pick elected officials and ultimately our first Black President.*

NAACP Freedom Rally
Pictured below are:
Mr. Rosemore Boyd, *President, Canton Branch, NAACP*
Father Luke Mikschl, *Parish Priest, Holy Child Jesus School*
Mr. Roy Wilkins, *National President, NAACP, New York City, New York.*

"Ballot from Freedom Vote"

FREEDOM VOTE

November 3, 1963

(This is an un-official Ballot)

Mark One Choice With An X

FOR GOVERNOR:

Aaron E. Henry [X]

Paul B. Johnson [ ]

Rubel Phillips [ ]

FOR LT. GOVERNOR:

Carrol Gartin [ ]

Edwin King [X]

Stanford Morse [ ]

In the early 1960's, Mr. Rosemore Boyd, reorganized the Madison County Branch of the Canton NAACP. By the spring of 1964, he officially reopened the NAACP office on Peace Street. This was ironic and historic. It was historic in that the office was opened on the main street of downtown Canton. Some years back, the NAACP was quite active in Canton and Madison County. In the 1940s, The Reverend L. S. Johnson was president. Due to constant death threats, reprisals and the strict enforcement of the "Jim Crow" laws, the NAACP was forced to shut down, Rev. Johnson was beaten and consequently was forced to leave Canton, in fear of his life. Many years later, he returned to his hometown of Canton to be with family in his latter years.

Copies of newspaper articles from The Associated Press and the United Press International, 1965

Blasts Rock Negro Church, Home In Canton

CANTON, Miss. (AP)—Explosions rocked a Negro church and a Negro home early Friday in this central Mississippi town which has been the target of increased civil rights activity in recent months.

There were no injuries.

Windows were shattered in both the Pleasant Green Church of Christ, used by civil rights workers for rallies; and the nearby home of Alberta Robertson.

Wilbur Robinson of the National Association for the Advancement of Colored People and George Raymond of the Congress of Racial Equality said the explosions were apparently caused by "chemical bombs."

Holes 12 inches in diameter and 5 inches deep were left on the lawns of both the church and Robertson woman's home, they said.

CORE initiated the voter campaign here and is cooperating now in the project with the NAACP and other civil rights groups, as well as the National Council of Churches.

Canton, 40 miles north of Jackson, is in Madison County, where Negroes outnumber whites nearly 7-3.

More Canton Bomb Blasts Are Reported

CANTON (UPI) — Authorities confirmed Friday that early morning explosions at a Negro church and home were being investigated.

Police Chief Dan Thomas would not comment except to say his department was checking out reports from civil rights groups.

The Council of Federated Organizations (COFO), which has sponsored a Negro voter registration campaign here, said no one was injured in either of the blasts, but windows were knocked out of both the church and home.

A COFO spokesman charged the explosions were caused by bombs tossed onto the lawns of the pleasant green church and a nearby home occupied by Mrs. Alberta Robinson.

The church, where civil rights rallies have been conducted, was not heavily damaged, the spokesman said. The only apparent damage was broken windows.

The COFO worker said a small hole was blasted in the lawn at the Robinson Home.

A similar explosion last week shattered a window at the "freedom House" sleeping quarters of civil rights workers. No injuries were reported

It was ironic there was so little peace on a street called Peace. It was on Peace Street that Black citizens marched for and attempted to exercise our rights. It was on Peace Street that white citizens strongly resisted our efforts. They controlled the Madison County Court House, the County Registrar's Office, the Mayor and Sheriff's Offices and City Hall, all on Peace Street. The newly opened NAACP office was located within one block of these establishments, all on Peace Street. Black citizens felt such a sense of pride knowing about the success of Mr. Boyd's accomplishment. After all, he negotiated the rental office space from a local sympathetic white merchant, one who supported our cause.

As I became more active in the movement, one day after speaking at a mass meeting the night before, Mr. Boyd came to my mom's home to ask if I would come to work for the NAACP. I did not give him a definite answer at that time, because I needed time to ponder this request. I had to think of all of the ramifications of this decision. My children and my parents had to be considered. The issue of our safety was very real. There was much more than my own safety to consider. I was personally not afraid, however, I was reluctant to take on a public role. My presence in the NAACP office meant that I would be highly visible and in the center of much activity. The office itself had high visibility. After a couple of weeks, I decided that I would accept this challenge.

In a very short time, we were notified that Ms. Gertrude Gorhman of the National Office of the NAACP in New York City, was being sent to assist Mr. Boyd in structuring the tasks of the office. She was tiny, energetic, knowledgeable, fearless, an excellent mentor, organizer and trainer for us. It was my responsibility to find housing for Ms. Gorhman.

The following Sunday at church, I asked Mrs. Mary Louise Adams who had housed civil rights workers in the past, if Ms. Gorhman could stay in her home. She said she needed time to think about it. Actually, we didn't have a lot of time. Ms. Gorhman was on her way. She arrived the very next day. I took her to the Adams' home where she was welcomed. So began our marathon. Every day Ms. Gorhman had a prepared agenda. Mrs. Adams joined us, and the three of us surveyed almost every home in Canton to determine the number of potential voters. With the help of many other local people, we went door-to-door trying to get people to register. While many of our people wanted to register and vote, they were simply afraid. They were aware of many horror stories against activists.

Blacks had a potential of more than 10,000, but yet only about 100 were registered. They were mostly ministers and school teachers which posed no threat to the white establishment. Canton was flooded with many young white freedom workers. They had come from all over the country into several Mississippi counties to help with voter registration.

They stayed in homes of local people as well as the "Freedom House" owned by Mr. and Mrs. George Washington, Sr. Although many of those who housed these young people were threatened, I know of no instance where local people turned these volunteers away.

Freedom was in the blood and nothing could stop it. We were a people whose time had come.

One day I received a call from Charles Evers, then State Field Secretary of the NAACP. He informed me that twelve students from LaMoyne College in Syracuse, New York, were on their way to Canton. Mr. Evers was the brother of and successor to his slain brother, Medgar Evers. He had come to Mississippi immediately from Chicago to carry on Medgar's work. The students would be staying for six weeks. I was asked to find housing for them. With such short notice, that was quite a challenge. I called Mrs. Mozell Lee, who readily accepted four. That left eight to be placed. My options were few; they stayed with us. Today, I still wonder how I housed those students along with my three children in my home on Boyd Street, but we managed. They soon learned to eat black-eyed and crowder peas; cornbread, chicken stew and other ethnic and regional foods. Many community people brought food each day to help me feed these students.

Students from LaMoyne College in our home, 1964

We worked all day knocking on doors, walking the dusty streets of Canton and attending nightly mass meetings. Our volunteers learned the 21-item questionnaire so they could assist in preparing prospective registered voters. They took local citizens to the Registrar's Office and encouraged them when they were turned away, as they most often were.

Any break in the evening routine was an opportunity for fellowship. All the students gathered on my front porch where we would sing freedom songs. One of the students brought a guitar with him. They taught us their songs. We taught them ours. It was a learning experience for us all.

One of the things I did in an effort to ensure their safety was to take all of them to the local sheriff's office. I advised him who these students were, what they would be doing and that I was responsible for them. I emphasized that I did not want any problems from his department. If there were any complaints regarding them or their activities, I was to be contacted immediately. There were to be absolutely no exceptions.

Many times I arrived at the NAACP office to find several cards under the door advising me that, *"The Eyes of the Klan are upon you."* The first few times that I found the cards, I was a little concerned, but not afraid to the extent that I was going to stop my activity. That and other fear tactics did not work.

Through a lot of prayer, I tried, to the best of my ability, to prepare myself for possible and eminent danger. Threatening phone calls were received daily, both in the office, and at our home. White men in trucks with exposed and filled gun racks followed me continually. I was never really afraid

for myself, but as I remembered Emmett Till and the four little girls in Birmingham, I was mostly concerned for my children. Their lives were also threatened. To protect them, I followed them home from school each day by driving on another street until they arrived home safely. I did not tell them this until more than 30 years later. I wanted to maintain a sense of normalcy for them and not one of them being fearful.

Young people attended many of our night meetings with their parents, who were afraid to leave them home alone. Their energy needed direction. As a musician, I thought of organizing a youth choir to sing at the meetings. I contacted the Pleasant Green Church and once again, they opened their doors to us. Their parents were very supportive as I knew all of them. The kids were so excited. The choir would keep them off the street and at the same time, this would give them something positive to do, including learning about our history. They learned to sing all of the "freedom songs" and sang at rallies and meetings all over the state.

They won many awards. The choir was organized and named for Mr. Vernon Dahmer of Hattiesburg, who had been killed when his home was firebombed. Mr. Dahmer was President of the Hattiesburg Branch of the NAACP and a community activist. As I attended his funeral and visited their burned out home, my dedication, as well as my determination, grew even stronger. I was convinced, more than ever, that the decision to be involved in the movement was the right one. The choir sang at many functions. Just as Mrs. Myrlie Evers had become a widow, now Mrs. Jewel Dahmer had also. A sad and hurtful sight was to watch their four sons stand at their childhood burned out home the day of his funeral. They were all dressed in various military uniforms and serving our country while hatred killed their father and injured their sister.

The Vernon Dahmer Singers for Freedom, 1966

Our musician was 15 year old Henry Myers, Jr. (now deceased)

Some of their favorite songs were; "If you miss me from the back of the bus and you can't find me no where, come on up to the front of the bus, and I'll be driving up there"

"Peace Be Still"

"Something's Got a Hold On Me"

"O, Freedom", "Woke up this morning with my mind, stayed on Freedom"

And of course the civil rights Anthem, "We Shall Overcome!"

Chapter 4
Canton ~ The Heat of the Night

I continued to work for the Canton Branch of the NAACP through 1966. My salary was $25.00 a week. Because of where the office was located, a variety of civil rights activities took place there. The possibility of danger was always present. My mom and dad were concerned about my safety, but their faith assured them I would be alright. I was often in the office alone; but many people from the community would call and stop by to check on me. We regularly received threatening and obscene telephone calls. White males, filled with hatred and brandishing their shotguns, would ride by and often give me the "half of a peace sign." Some would even park their trucks in front of the NAACP office as well as my home on Boyd Street and just sit for long periods of time. Again, **NO** fear.

One day Attorney Jack Young, Sr., one of my mentors from my year in the Biloxi Café came to Canton to speak at one of our night rallies. I took him to my parent's home for dinner. During the course of our conversation, I asked him to reassure Mom that I was going to be alright, and that nothing was going to happen to me.

His resounding reply was straight and to the point. He said, *"I wish that I could give her that assurance, but I can't."* He then turned to me and said: *"You are involved in many activities which have the potential for danger. It is possible that something could happen to you."*

For the first time, I found myself questioning my involvement in the movement. Quickly, I thought about what would happen to my children if something happened to me? I began recounting the obscene telephone calls. I remembered calls which not only threatened my life, but the safety of my children. I remembered other acts of intimidation including the "Klan Cards". Although I was able to keep my concerns from Attorney Young and Mom, I was a "little bit" afraid. There were times I was so afraid, I really didn't know just how afraid I really was. In spite of my fear, we attended the rally, my work continued.

When I returned home, the Lord and I had a really serious encounter. He brought me back to our initial conversation. He assured me, **"I am with you, you've got to GO!!"** After that discussion, even though I had some very tense moments, the fear was gone. I was never afraid again. If anything, this spiritual experience energized me and helped me to focus on my commission. I was not a quitter; my work continued with renewed dedication. Through the years of my advocacy, His promise has remained. He has kept me safe in the face of present and constant danger.

*Volunteers assisting prospective voters on the use of
the 21 item Voter Registration Questionnaire*

So many people from the North wanted to assist in the struggle. Some were able to come as volunteers. Those who could not come assisted by sending books, money and clothing. There were so many boxes, Barbara Boyd, the daughter of Mr. & Mrs. Rosemore Boyd, and secretary of the local chapter, Mrs. Adams and I worked many hours sorting the items for distribution to people in the community.

Cathy Cade came from Philadelphia, PA., to help in the struggle

People from across the county came to the NAACP office and the Freedom House to pick up leaflets and information on registering and voting. They wanted information about the newly passed Civil Rights Bill, precinct information, freedom meeting schedules and the whole range of local and state activities.

Citizens often complained about the treatment they received when they attempted to register and to vote. Complaints ranged from being required to wait for nearly an hour while whites came in and registered immediately. Keep in mind that Blacks still had to complete the 21-item questionnaire. They also complained how rudely they were treated, how they were yelled at, cursed at, arbitrarily put out of the Registrar's office and turned down as they attempted to interpret the Constitution.

Many attempts were made to meet with the Registrar in an effort to "soften" the treatment that Blacks were receiving. The Registrar was quite candid in expressing his feelings about **Blacks** or *"Nigras"* as he frequently called us. Other attempts were made to meet with local Supervisors, the Chancery Clerk and both County and City Attorneys. While some of them empathized, we all understood that the Registrar, L. Foote Campbell, "ran his office" as he saw fit.

After many attempts to rectify this situation locally, our final recourse was to seek federal intervention.

An unidentified source provided us a copy of the 21-item Questionnaire. Receiving this document was a major victory. Having access to this information speeded our ability to better prepare our people for the registration process. Copies were shared and distributed among local civil rights groups. Several strategies were used to ensure the participation of potential Black voters. It was still important to protect the identity of persons willing to risk their involvement. For those persons, local organizers went door-to-door teaching them how to answer the questions as opposed to in a public mass freedom meeting.

For those prospective voters who felt more comfortable in a larger group setting, a series of workshops were conducted throughout the county. Their focus centered not only on the questionnaire, but also on other current community issues. Despite our teaching sessions and words of encouragement, our people knew they would be alone when they actually faced the Registrar. We could prepare them for the preliminaries, but none of us knew which section of the Constitution they would be required to interpret. As I look back on this, it all seems so long ago, but thirty years (at the time of this writing in 1994), is really not a long time in comparison to the length of time that we as Blacks have been denied our rights guaranteed under the Constitution.

I had the opportunity at the request of Representative Charles Diggs to testify in Congressional Hearings to send Federal Examiners to Mississippi to oversee voter registration. Elected to the House of Representatives in 1954 at age 31, Charles C. Diggs, Jr., was the first African American to represent Michigan in Congress. Our efforts were successful. Many Examiners came to help us. I am standing outside of the office of Attorney General Robert Kennedy.

As the intensity of racist practices increased in Canton, we were forced to take action. A number of community organizations, including the NAACP, petitioned for the intervention from the United States Department of Justice and the Office of the Attorney General, Robert Kennedy. We sent telegrams, wrote letters, made telephone calls and others traveled to Washington to meet with the Kennedys: President and Attorney General.

This flurry of activity provided several of us with the opportunity to participate in hearings in Washington, D. C. We carried with us many documented cases of voter discrimination. The influence of Mr. Roy Wilkins, Executive Director of the NAACP and other national leaders to whom we had also appealed for help prompted Attorney General Robert Kennedy to send federal examiners to Canton. Mr. Kennedy's office called the Canton NAACP office and informed me of his decision.

The arrival of the federal examiners signaled that our efforts were victorious and the end of intimidation of Blacks in the Registrar's office. This would also eliminate the dreaded 21-item questionnaire. This was the beginning of a new day of hope and optimism for our people.

When the examiners came to open the office, there were approximately 152 Blacks registered in the entire county. Our voting potential was approximately 10,366 Black citizens. The county was 70% Black.

Many Blacks came in to make inquiries, but most were hesitant at first, to actually register. The fear of reprisal and retaliation continued to be very real. We had been successful in securing the presence of the federal examiners whose primary purpose of being in Canton was to conduct voter registration. Their continued presence was contingent on our efforts to convince citizens to come into the office and register. This meant our efforts had to be intensified. All groups answered the call.

We would have to visit more homes. We organized and scheduled more community meetings throughout the county. We distributed more leaflets. We made many more personal contacts to encourage our citizens to use the services of the federal examiners. Announcements were sent to those churches which had been supportive of our efforts from the beginning. We posted leaflets in Black-owned business, we did it all AGAIN.

We contacted other churches which had not been as actively involved. Speaking teams were sent to those churches and to an expanded group of many community organizations. We established car pools. We knocked on more doors, visited more home; some three or more times. All of these efforts, particularly the involvement of the Black churches in the community, turned the tides. Finally, our people had a clear vision of what had to be done and what power we have when we worked together.

Jackson Daily News, 1965

Suit Filed In Madison Vote Drive

[handwritten: March 6]
[handwritten: Jackson paper]

United Press International

The Justice Department Thursday filed suit to halt alleged voter registration discrimination against Negroes in Madison County, where a registration drive is in progress.

The suit was filed as a class action on behalf of all Negro adults in the county, and named L. F. Campbell, the Madison County Circuit Court clerk and registrar.

SATURDAY

A hearing on a motion for a temporary restraining order was set for Saturday in Federal District Court here.

The suit charged that Campbell has processed Negro applications on a one-at-a-time basis while handling applications of whites on a simultaneous basis. Affidavits filed with the suit said several hundred Negroes stood in line to register last Friday and Saturday but only seven were processed.

The affidavits charged that Campbell has registered as many as 49 whites per day in the past.

OTHER CHARGES

The complaint also charged that Negro applicants have been forced to meet more stringent standards, have been discouraged from attempting to register, have been denied registration and have been rejected though qualified.

Kennedy said the complaint was filed only after the government was unable to resolve the problems through consultations with local officials.

The Justice Department said there are about 10,366 adult Negroes in Madison County, of whom about 152 are registered. More than 5,000 of the 5,622 adult whites in the county are registered.

Ask Federal Intervention

[handwritten: May 29]

CANTON, Miss. (Special) — A civil rights organization today called for "immediate intervention" by the federal government following arrests of 55 persons and clubbing of one during voter registration marches here Friday.

McKinley Hamilton, 24, of near Canton, was treated at a hospital for minor injuries received when he was struck by a policeman. He was jailed after treatment.

Police charged he cursed an officer.

A total of 55 persons were arrested on charges of parading without a permit, including four white representatives of the National Council of Churches.

Arrests came when Negroes attempted to march in groups from a Negro area to the courthouse. Police blocked the marchers, telling them they could go in pairs or one at a time, the same rules which Negroes abided during a February "freedom day" here.

The Council of Federated Organizations, which directed the voter drive, sent telegrams to President Lyndon B. Johnson and Atty. Gen. Robert Kennedy demanding "immediate intervention to obtain full medical care and prevent further such incidents."

Negroes stood in line at the courthouse, filing registration applications four at a time. The civil rights organization said 42 applied during the day.

The word spread rapidly that the federal examiners were in Canton. Within a week or so, the examiners were so busy, that they had to call for additional back-up assistance. They also had to extend their hours daily. As Black registrants entered the federal examiners' office, they were treated with utmost respect. They received the same six-item questionnaire as did our white counterparts. For the first time, local residents felt valued and validated as first-class citizens. As a result, several thousand Blacks came to register in preparation for voting. Fortunately, the NAACP office was only two doors from that of the Federal Examiners.

I visited the office of the examiners several times across the day. The visits were not only to reinforce the confidence of local residents who happened to be there registering, but also to receive the official count of the numbers of persons who registered for that day. We knew then that our collective efforts were paying off. The office was not only a safe haven for our citizens, but their presence was a major accomplishment for Madison County.

To see the expressions on the faces of the newly registrants reassured us that our cause was right. One day, an elderly lady came up to me with tears in her eyes. She said, " *been wanting to do this all of my life, but Mam, I was scared. I finally got my civil rights!*" We hugged and cried together. The next day she called and asked us to come and pick up all of the persons in her household. We did and all eight were registered. There were many instances where similar acts like this occurred. One person would come in to register, soon to be followed by an entire household. This feeling was the same as, "gettin' new religion."

Once our people "caught the vision", they were not afraid of seeing their names in the local newspaper. They were not afraid of losing their jobs. In fact, many of them did. They were not afraid of being threatened, jailed or even beaten. In fact, many were. This "freedom thing" was catching on. More than anything, Blacks felt hope and a sense of pride. We made the movement work. We knew we were as good as anybody, regardless of our race, our social status, our economic condition, where we lived, or who our folks were. Finally, we felt empowered and a part of the process.

This level of enthusiasm continued well after the federal examiners left. Blacks began to talk about running for public office and running for various city and county seats. In 1967, Mr. U. S. Rimmer, from Camden, was the first Black elected to a local judgeship in Beat 5, Madison County. That same year, Mr. Fred Singleton and Mr. Frank Williams ran though unsuccessfully, for other county-wide offices. Other Blacks who became actively involved as candidates included: Mrs. Betty Robinson, Rev. Clifton Goodloe, Jr., Mr. Arthur Tate and others. For the first time, we felt that we really could elect persons who represented the 70% majority Black county's population. To quote Dr. King, "we're on the move now".

The price Mr. and Mrs. Tate paid for his active involvement was the loss of his job with the Canton Public School system. Although these three candidates were defeated and we were disappointed, we were not discouraged. This only intensified our efforts to work even harder. We knew hard work would pay off, because later, Rev. Clifton Goodloe (my brother-in-law), became the first Black to serve as Chairman of the School Board for Madison County. Mr. Tate was elected in 1979 as the first African American Senator since reconstruction.

During this period, there were all out efforts to integrate such "white-only" facilities as the swimming pool, the movie theater, local restaurants and other segregated institutions. There were more marches, more meetings, more demonstrations. One hot summer day a group of Blacks and whites marched to the "white only" swimming pool. Eleven of the demonstrators were arrested, but follow-up attempts were made immediately and continuously. Even the "black" only swimming pool was closed in an attempt to make us retreat and give up our quest for full access to public tax payer funded facilities. .

Led by C. O. Chinn, Jr., black and white demonstrators attempt to integrate the local white only swimming pool. Youth from the Vernon Dahmer Choir integrated the local white only movie theatre. We were bombarded with gum, popcorn, "spit balls", taunts, jeers and much more.

By court-order, Black citizens ordered use of the local Canton Park

Canton Ordered To Allow Negroes Use Of Park

A federal judge Monday ordered officials at Canton, Miss., to permit Negroes the same use of a city park as that extended white residents of the area.

U. S. District Judge Harold Cox granted a temporary injunction sought by a group of civil rights workers. The order enjoined officials from arresting or otherwise seeking to block Negroes from using the park and its facilities.

Cox said the plaintiffs would suffer "immediate and irreparable injuries by being prevented from engaging in activities protected by the 14th Amendment to the Constitution" unless the order was issued.

Negroes and whites who filed the suit claimed a group of whites tried to run them down with a pickup truck when they entered the park June 17. They

day after the court action was filed, and 11 were arrested by city police on charges of trespassing.

They were trying to use swings and park benches when arrested.

Cox's injunction named as defendants Canton's city officials, Sheriff Jack S. Cauthen. the Canton Department of Parks and Recreation, park director Lonus Hucks. and their agents.

The order also was directed at "John" (first name not known) Peterson, charged in the suit with leading the intimidation on June 17. He was enjoined from "attempting to or threatening, harassing, intimidating or injuring the Negroes."

Canton and county officials were prohibited from any action to stop Negroes from using the park "under the same con-

20 JACKSON DAILY NEW

Negroes See Ball Game Of Canton Whites

No Incidents But Jeers After Court Grants Injunction

CANTON. Miss. (UPI) —Civil rights workers said local Negroes desegregated the city park here Tuesday without incident except for a few jeers from whites.

A Federal judge had directed city officials not to arrest or otherwise interfere with Negroes

Mr. George Washington. Sr., at 77, first to take a swim in the newly re-opened pool.

1984

There were many instances which show the depth to which patterns of discrimination were entrenched, occurred in my immediate family. My father, who is now a licensed plumber and electrician, had work taken from him by local whites who tried to coerce him into "stopping me", as they would say. This happened countless times. On one occasion, he was in the midst of a big job and was told, in no uncertain terms, that if he did not stop my involvement in all of this "civil rights mess", he would be fired. My father lived his values as he continues to do so today. We had been taught by him and mom to stand up for what we believed in.

As a result, he told the gentleman, "Sir, my daughter is a grown woman with children, I do not dictate her activity. If you choose to take this job from me because of her, then you have to do that." My father was fired. I felt very bad; but he encouraged me not to feel guilty.

Dad: For your inspiration and love, I am proud to be your daughter. I shall always be guided by your courageous spirit. You have taught us the value of hard work through your example, I only hope I can follow in your foot-steps.

I remember another instance. In the 1950's, when my dad first applied for his electrician, butane and plumbers' licenses. If successful, he would become Canton's first Black to obtain a triple license. He was required to take the test on three different occasions. He was turned down each time. The tests were rescheduled at the city's discretion, in the Court Room. Mom's support was unwavering. She encouraged him to persist and return each time the test was scheduled. The third time he went to take the test, a young white lad was assigned to watch him to be sure he was not copying or did not have hidden notes in his sleeves. After the third attempt and the personal intervention of a white merchant, he was licensed. A couple of years later, the white Superintendent of the department actually admitted that Dad passed the test each time, but that the City of Canton was not ready to license a "Colored". Long since that time, many things have changed. Now, my father serves as Vice-president of the Board which licenses all plumbers, Black and white. He also assists in inspecting jobs for the City. But again, someone had to be the first, even though that was not his intent. As others took work from my father, he was undaunted in his resolve to maintain his manhood. Because he was he best, jobs were later restored. *Fast Forward*: **Sixty years later, that space was dedicated as** *The Flonzie Brown Goodloe Court Room* **& accepted in my parents honor.**

I remember so well one hot Wednesday afternoon. My young cousin, Vatrice Goodloe came to the NAACP Office to report that she had attempted to be served at the "white only" window of the local ice cream parlor. As was the practice, she was turned away and then directed to the "Colored only" window located on the side of the building. My first thought was, "Do our young people also have to be subjected to these insane and discriminatory acts? **"When will it end?"** After all, this was an innocent teenager who only wanted an ice-cream cone. I became so incensed that Vatrice and I returned and in my less than conciliatory tone, I demanded to be served and after a series of looks and a quick attitude adjustment by the owner, we were served at the "white only" window.

In 1966, I began working for an anti-poverty program titled Systematic Training And Redevelopment, Incorporated (STAR, Inc.). STAR was a literacy program funded by the Office of Economic Opportunity (OEO). It was sponsored by the state-wide Catholic Diocese and was housed locally in the Canton Parish under the leadership of Fr. Luke Mikschl. The goal of the project was to assist citizens in attaining their GED Certificate. While most of the persons who attended were Black, the program was opened to all. After several months, a few local whites participated. Since I was familiar with the layout and demographics of the city and the county, I was hired as a recruiter. Fortunately, this position was one which allowed me to continue a high level of involvement in the community.

It was difficult for me to get used to the fact that I was actually now getting paid to do work that I had volunteered for those years. That was hard to believe. There were many of us former volunteers who finally became employed within Head Start, STAR and a few other social programs. Although our salaries were menial at best, we were grateful to have some income. In fact, there were times when we felt that someone else should have held those jobs. Our employment encouraged us to work harder in lobbying for those in the trenches who were still unemployed.

The late 1960's was the era of anti-poverty legislation. This legislation provided monies to support the development and implementation of community-based programs. It took several years for these dollars to trickle down to those of us on the front lines in Mississippi. The Governor and other state officials consistently blocked any attempts to be awarded federal dollars. They refused to allocate state monies which were required as matching funds. Their refusal constituted a shameful attempt to maintain the status quo. They did not want Black citizens to have access to these dollars. These resources would force the acceptance of equity in employment and would eradicate the legal forms of discrimination and eventually curtail other forms of institutionalized racism.

Chapter 5

Trodding Unchartered Waters

VOTE NOV 5th FOR **(Mrs.) Flonzie GOODLOE** Election Commission Madison County Beat 1

Ten Qualify In Race For Election Commissioners

Ten candidates qualified to run for the office of Election Commissioner in Madison County, according to W. A. Sims, Clerk of the Board of Supervisors. The ten will appear on the Nov. 5 ballot in conjunction with the presidential election.

One commissioner will be elected from each beat in the county, but the candidates will be voted on at large. Each candidate must reside in the district in which he runs.

Candidates include, in Beat One, Sim Dulaney, Tom Riddell, and Mrs. Flonzie Goodloe; Beat Two, James A. Tanner and Ben Childress; Beat Three, P. W. Bozeman; Beat Four, Emerson Crosby, Clifton Renfroe and W. E. Garrett; Beat Five, Mrs. Mary C. Draper.

In the past, election commissioners have been appointed by the governor. Due to a bill passed by the State Legislature in March of this year, however, the commissioners will now be elected at large by the counties they serve.

The commissioners elected in November will assume office Jan. 1, 1969. The County Board of Supervisors will continue to carry out the duties of election commissioners, as they have done since the new law was passed and the old board of commissioners was abolished in August.

Election commissioners assume much of the responsibilities for carrying out elections, regardless of the primary or political party involved. They certify candidates, arrange for ballots and appoint poll workers.

Voters in the Madison County Separate School District will also elect two members to the County School Board. Edward L. Henderson will be elected at large, and Harold H. White, Jr. is the candidate in District Two.

In 1968, the County Election Commissioner's position and other county positions became available. I never thought of running for public office. Others believed that I could be a viable candidate. One night at a mass meeting, Mrs. Annie Devine, a veteran of the early days, approached me and told me that a number of community people had met and I had been slated to run for the position. I looked at her with surprise and a crazy kind of an expression. (Today, we often laugh as we still remember the look on my face.) I replied saying, "I respect the opinions of the community, but I am really not interested." I didn't know the law and I did not want to be a failure. The next time she saw me, she looked me squarely in the face, pointed her finger and said, **"Flonzie, you will run for this position, you don't have a choice, you have to do this."**

After a few days, Mrs. Devine and I talked again and I consented to run for the position of Election Commissioner. The fear this time was that I would not meet the expectations of those who were counting on me. I knew I was a committed worker. The leadership requirements for this task seemed awesome. I was again assured of God's promise.

In 1968, Madison County had five Beats and thirteen precincts. It was my understanding that each Beat had its own individual Election Commissioner. I soon learned I would be running as an at-large candidate from Canton which was Beat 1. My votes not only had to be drawn from Canton, but also from the other twelve Precincts throughout the county. In our opinion, the procedure was voter-suppression and blatant discrimination, to say the least. Prior to my candidacy, candidates only had to run from within their Beats. I had to garner votes from the entire 13 precinct county areas. We concluded this to be yet another deterrent to discourage us. It did not work! On the other hand, these challenges sounded very familiar. Had we not been organized and registered in significant numbers in the county at that time, their last minute and arbitrary at-large rule could have cost us the election. This was the first county-wide election in which Black citizens had participated in large numbers. Even as we determined the procedure to be discriminatory, we realized that many other challenges were yet to be faced.

Since I was working in a federally funded program, I had to run as an Independent. That proved to be another hurdle. We had to work harder. We had to produce and distribute more fliers. I had to campaign in each of the 13 precincts. My campaign required more work, in fact, more time, more travel, more resources, more of everything. In retrospect, if there was any one thing that united the county and gave us hope, it was my election. I was on the ticket with Presidential candidate Hubert Humphrey. We both won in Madison County. These challenges inspired us to work even harder and it paid off. **I had actually won!!**

There was much jubilation on the evening of November 5, 1968, when it was confirmed that I had actually won the Election Commissioner's post. I was the first Black and female to be elected to a county-wide public office in the bi-racial town of Canton, Madison County and Mississippi; post or pre-Reconstruction. (Except Mound Bayou). Father Luke Mikschl prepared a celebration at the gymnasium of the Holy Child Jesus Catholic Church. People came from all over the county to share in this historic event. Mr. W. E. Garrett was also elected as a first Black male Election Commissioner. His area of responsibility was only in Beat 4, the Farmhaven community, which is ironically, my birthplace. There was good reasons to celebrate. Our victories represented hope. Our victories represented what could be done when people focused their energies and worked together in unity as well as a beginning of an end to blatant voter discrimination in Madison County.

CANTON, MISSISSIPPI, THURSDAY, NOVEMBER 7, 1968 — Cents Per Copy—Vol. 76 No. 45

Madison County Herald

Humphrey Carries County; Goodloe Defeats Riddell

Hubert H. Humphrey has carried Madison County, in a day of political upset.

One of the biggest upsets locally was the defeat of Democrat Tom H. Riddell, Jr., who lost the District One Election Commissioner's race to Independent Flonzie Goodloe. Riddell served as chairman of the Madison County Election Commission under the old appointive system, which was abolished in August.

Humphrey's and Mrs. Goodloe's wins were sparked by heavy majorities in the West Ward. Both victories were attributed to heavy Negro registration, and to an unusually heavy Negro voter turnout.

Some 8800 of Madison County's 14,628 registered voters cast ballots, equalling a voting turnout of approximately 60 per cent—better than in previous years, but still not good.

The election commissioner race gave Flonzie Goodloe 3,613 to Riddell's 3,591. In District Four, Independent candidate W. E. Garrett polled 3,685 votes to win over Republican Emerson Crosby, with 2,094. In the three remaining districts, Democrats P. W. Bozeman and Mrs. Mary Draper, and Republican Ben Childress ran without opposition.

Madison County joined the Fourth Congressional District in giving a solid endorsement to incumbent Congressman G. V. "Sonny" Montgomery, who polled 4,221 votes to win over challenger Prentiss Walker, 1,298.

Supreme Court Justice Henry Lee Rodgers ran without opposition.

In other county races, Independent candidate Carl R. Mason was elected constable for District Two, with 452 votes to Democrat Jimmie M. Dykes' 167. Edwin L. Henderson and Harold H. White, Sr., were unopposed for seats on the County School Board.

The proposed constitutional amendment was soundly defeated in Madison County, by vote of 3,167 to 1,346. State returns indicated a defeat for the amendment, which would have removed highway bonds from the state's limited bonded indebtedness.

The vote was not good enough for George Wallace, former governor of Alabama, the third party candidate expected to carry the county. He trailed Democrat Humphrey, who received 4,222 votes in Madison County, to Wallace's 3,858. Republican Richard Nixon ran a poor third with 801 county votes.

Humphrey polled more votes in the three city wards than did Wallace and Nixon together. Humphrey's total in the North, South and West Wards was 2,553; and Wallace and Nixon together polled 2,395. Approximately 7,834 voters are registered in the city, and of these 4,948 or about 63 per cent voted in the presidential election—again, better than usual, but not good.

All the above returns are complete, with all of Madison County's 13 precincts reporting; but are unofficial. Official figures will be released after certification by the acting Election Commission, the Madison County Board of Supervisors.

In the early hours of the next morning, I was awakened by a telephone call. The caller chose to remain anonymous. The time of the call was not surprising. Since my appointment as Branch Director of the Canton NAACP office, threatening telephone calls came regularly, most often throughout the night. This one, however, was different. The caller did not give his name nor did I recognize his voice. He simply said, *"I am happy that you won. I will be working with you and I will watch your back. I have heard that you are fair-minded and I am looking forward to working with you. He said further, that in addition to himself, I had received a number of white votes."* Because the white male incumbent occupied that position for many years, I was amazed at his revelation. I wasn't sure how to interpret his call; nor was I sure if this was just a prank. I just thanked him for his call. I learned later that the caller was white and a member of the Election Commission. He honored his word.

UNOFFICIAL RETURNS — General Election Nov. 5, 1968

After having some time to analyze the results of the election, I knew I had gotten white votes. It took some time for all of the events of the campaign to really sink in. It took time for me to realize that I was now an elected official of Madison County, the first in a bi-racial Mississippi town and an Agent of the State of Mississippi. I was not to officially take office until January 20, 1969. This gave me time to really study the law and become more familiar with Madison County politics--establishment style.

To say the least, the next four years were quite eventful. One of my first priorities was to actually review the voter registration books, page by page and book by book. For years, it was common knowledge that the names of persons who had voted might have been arbitrarily scratched off the record. Many times I had accompanied persons to the voting places and had seen instances where their names had been marked out with the words "deceased", "moved", "invalid", etc., having been substituted. I was determined to search the records to authenticate these erroneous strike overs. Even though it took some time, I accomplished that goal.

My other priorities were to appoint voters to work at the polls who represented a broad segment of the County's population and also to conduct voter education and training sessions for new voters.

The first time the Commission met, we extended courtesies to each other and vowed to work together for the betterment of the county. We each expressed what our goals were. We also identified some of the problems. As we began the actual preparation for elections, I was immediately faced with two major challenges. I had to engage in battle with the three white Commissioners on a variety of issues on several occasions. My first challenge was seeking agreement to qualify Black candidates.

The first person to present a qualifying petition for certification was Mr. Herman Burrell, a Black candidate from Beat 5. It was my contention that Mr. Burrell's petition contained the necessary prerequisites for certification. After much discussion, when it came time to vote on his eligibility, I was defeated. The Election Board was comprised of five individuals--three whites and two Blacks. Voting nearly always proceeded along racial lines. Mr. W. E. Garrett and I always voted in concert. He also knew first-hand the extent of voter-registration complaints from Blacks in his Beat. I felt so strongly about the rightness of my vote that I was determined to seek further legal redress. At issue was the validity of the signatures of qualified voters whose names appeared on the candidate's petition. Mr. Burrell's petition had been denied many, many times.

The most blatant examples of this form of voter discrimination were instances where qualified voters had been declared: "deceased, or moved, or not registered, or not voted in 5 years, all of which were untrue."

I can recall actually bringing people into the Commission meetings to verify their viability, their longevity and their addresses.

My colleagues continuously voted to deny Mr. Burrell's petition. With the assistance of Attorney George "Peachtree" Taylor, a civil rights lawyer from New York, I filed the necessary legal documents to prepare for a court decision. In this instance, the court ordered the Commission to certify Mr. Burrell's petition. He ran for office, won the position of Constable for Beat 5 and served for many, many years.

On at least four other occasions, I was forced to seek court intervention on matters pertaining to qualifying Black candidates. In each case, the judge upheld my position. In one instance, the judge ordered that a scheduled election be set aside until he could decide the merits of the argument. Prior to my election, we never knew with certainty why a candidate's petition failed to certify. Now that I was on the inside, I was quickly becoming familiar with the politics of the establishment. I was not intimidated and was determined to do right.

I concluded that a part of my task and responsibility as a first recognized Black elected official in the state was to fight the arbitrary nature of the decisions which kept Blacks from qualifying, running for office and winning county-wide positions. By the late sixties, the majority of registered voters in Madison County were Black. It seemed appropriate that Blacks should hold comparable county-wide elected positions.

The second most important challenge was identifying poll-workers who were representatives of the total community. To the majority white commissioners, some of our Black citizens that I presented were viewed as controversial. Their high level of activism had historically precluded their acceptance as poll-workers. I was determined to change this long standing practice. In preparation for elections, each Commissioner presented a listing of poll-workers from their respective Beats. As a county-wide Commissioner, I felt strongly that the workers should represent their individual Beats. I brought before the Commission names of those who represented the broader Canton community. Mr. Garrett and I reviewed and acted in good faith on the lists presented by each Commissioner. We reached an impasse when my list was presented as many were perceived as "trouble makers."

It was unacceptable to me that individuals would be excluded from this opportunity due to their involvement in community activities. Historically, grass roots community people were not appointed to work at the polls. I was determined to include a cross-section of citizens to occupy those positions. Off to court we went again and, **WE WON AGAIN!!**

After lengthy debates, including court intervention, all of my people were confirmed. Many years after my election, on occasions, when I visit Canton on election day, it pleases me to see persons I appointed during my tenure as Election Commissioner still performing their tasks at the polls.

My next challenge was to seek concurrence from the Commission to conduct voter-education classes in the community. After my election, the County installed voting machines in all of the precincts. There were many new voters who had never used a voting machine. Prior to this, paper ballots were used. It was important to me that there would be an adequate opportunity for new voters to learn this new process. The classes were opened to anyone who wanted to come, regardless of race. Public notices were run in the local paper announcing the classes.

After I adequately prepared for our first workshop in mid-October in 1969, community people numbered close to two-hundred. They came with eager anticipation to learn the new voter procedures. I did not anticipate any trouble; nor did I expect any problems, but both occurred.

In the midst of the training session, as participants were gathered around the table being instructed on the new voting procedures, the deputy jailer came in unannounced and took the sample voting machine from the table. The class watched in amazement. I became very angry. When I questioned his reasons, he stated, "I have to remove it because I am responsible for keeping the machines. After all, I have to get up early in the morning and check on *my* prisoners." I loudly protested his actions, but he took the machine anyway. His actions in no way discouraged me or those attending. Back to Court, **WE WON AGAIN.** Subsequent classes were conducted!

Workshop Disruption In Madison Is Charged

ATLANTA, Ga. (AP) — The Voter Education Project Thursday charged that a voter workshop in Canton, Miss., was disrupted by a Madison County, Miss., deputy sheriff.

The Atlanta-based organization, which said the incident occurred Wednesday, called on the U.S. Justice Department to launch an investigation and "put an immediate end to voting rights violations."

A statement issued by the VEP charged that a deputy sheriff confiscated a voting machine which was being demonstrated to newly-registered black voters.

It said the voter education workshop was being conducted by VEP field representatives using audio-visual techniques and that the session was coordinated by a local black elected official, Mrs. Flonzie Goodloe, a member of the local election commission.

The statement said Mrs. Goodloe had received approval and permission from the election board on Sept. 24 to use the election machine in the workshop and that a notice of the public meeting was printed in a local newspaper.

Madison County has been the scene of continued harrassment, intimidation and disruption as local whites and even public officials have sought to deny the vote to black citizens," charged VEP Executive Director John Lewis.

Madison County officials were not immediately available for comment on the charge.

Lewis termed the incident "shocking" and said it was "dramatic evidence that the Justice Department must do more to insure the rights of black citizens under the Voting Rights Act of 1965 . . .."

In Canton, Mrs. Goodloe said she did not think the incident was "any sort of conspiracy. Actually I think it was just the actions of one old man from the old school of thought who got fed up with negroes and white folks getting together. . . .

"Don't get me wrong," she said, "I think we definitely need a Justice Department representative because there has been harassement here and we have a large number of black candidates."

But, "I don't think the entire sheriff's office was involved. It was just too political and he was not going to have nothing to do with it."

Mrs. Goodloe said the jailer "kept grumbling about the time the machine had been on dis-play. He apparently called it

I immediately lodged an official complaint with the Election Commission. Unfortunately for all of us, the Commission was not scheduled to meet until after the election. By design and by the time the Commission responded to the complaint, the election was over. Clearly, in my judgment, the deputy sheriff was not acting on his own. I believed his actions represented the decisions of those who continued in their attempts to halt Black voter progress. Voter suppression, wouldn't you say?

I viewed this as an apparent effort to embarrass me and to damage my credibility with my constituents. This particular form of intimidation did not work either. The participants and I discussed the event. It was our collective resolve to continue to move ahead. There were many such instances of attempts to stop me from performing my duties. At these times, I was encouraged and inspired to continue by my family, many friends and supporters. Seeing my determination, the Commission agreed and future classes were scheduled.

THE NEW YORK TIMES, SUNDAY, JANUARY 11, 1970

Black Activists Confident of the Future

The New York Times (by Gary Settle)

ACTIVE IN MISSISSIPPI ECONOMICS AND POLITICS: Negroes who are working to further black interests in the state include, from the left, Frederick Banks, a lawyer from Jackson; Robert G. Clark, a state legislator; Mrs. Monette Travis, a community organizer, and Mrs. Flonzie Goodloe, one of two black members on Madison Co. Elections board.

Attorney Fred Banks was successful in being elected to a Circuit Judgeship in Jackson, Mississippi. Representative Robert Clark was elected in 1967 as the first Black member to the Sate Legislature. He still serves in that position. Mrs. Monette Travis-Watts remains active in her community of Ypsilanti, Michigan. Today, Mississippi has more Black elected officials than any other state in the country. Blacks hold a variety of city, county and state-wide positions. My election contributed significantly to these collective victories.

Voter-education class in session. After the shut-down, many more citizens attended these follow-up classes than the previous session.

Fast Forward: This photo is displayed in the new MS Two Museums, 2017

THE NEW YORK TIMES, TUESDAY, NOVEMBER 2, 1971

130 Lawyers Arrive to Observe Mississippi Voting

By THOMAS A. JOHNSON
Special to The New York Times

JACKSON, Miss., Nov. 1—More than 130 out of state lawyers woke up in mostly poor black homes this morning to a state that is in the middle of a bumper harvest and a promising hunting season, and is facing what many here are calling "the most important election of our times."

Arriving late yesterday, the lawyers—about half of whom are white—were briefed on state voting laws and then driven by local people to the homes of black families in the state's 82 counties. Tomorrow, the lawyers will serve as poll-watchers when 286 black candidates compete for elective offices in elections that range from local constables to Governor.

Rides to the Polls

In many white areas, it is only the newspaper, radio and television advertisements that talk about the upcoming elections. But there is a near frenzy of activity in black areas.

In Belzoni, a flat, hot Delta town, Benita Bolden, a 20-year-old Howard University zoology major, and six of her classmates conferred on last-minute details today on how to get elderly and ill voters as well as housewives to the polls.

Three busloads of Howard students made the 23-hour trip to Mississippi last week; since then, they have been joined by hundreds of black and white students.

Johnson Aides

Lester Hyman, an aide to Senator Edmund S. Muskie, Democrat of Maine, and William Weeks, an aide to Representative Paul N. McCloskey Jr., Republican of California, worked in Mississippi's palm tree-studded Gulf port area of Pass Christian and Biloxi, where the black Mayor of Fayette, Charles Evers, expects his strongest white support in his campaign for the Governor's office. His principal opponent is a white lawyer, William Waller, who is considered a moderate.

Mrs. Lizzie Carpenter, former press secretary to Mrs. Lyndon B. Johnson, campaigned in Sunflower and Bolivar Counties with Mrs. Fannie Lou Hamer, a candidate for the State Senate. And Edward Weisl Jr., a former Assistant Attorney General under President Johnson, flew here today to coordinate any complaints that the black candidates might have.

The campaign reminded many observers of the summer of 1964, when the Student Nonviolent Coordinating Committee and the Congress of Racial Equality brought hundreds of black and white college students, as well as lawyers and celebrities, into the state to help with voter registration and voter education. But Michael D. Shagan, a lawyer, noted a major difference: "Local people are making the decisions now. We are simply supporting them."

Mr. Shagan, who is 30 years old, is the general counsel for the Offtrack Betting Corporation in New York City. He is spending his vacation coordi-

nating the travel and accommodations for the lawyers in the Evers for Governor headquarters in downtown Jackson.

Mr. Evers's headquarters is busy from early morning until late at night, but many offices in black communities around the state are no less busy. In Madison County just north of Jackson, Mrs. Flonzie Goodloe joined other blacks in passing out sample paper ballots showing the names and identifying numbers of the 30 black candidates for county posts.

'Choose Your Official'

"And if you have any trouble," Mrs. Goodloe tells every one she meets, "you just tell a voting official you want someone to help you and you can choose your official—you can choose someone you know, someone you trust."

Much of the activity in black districts in recent days has centered on the methods of casting a vote, both by voting machines and by paper ballots. The Drummer, a weekly

newspaper published by the Poor Peoples Corporation in Jackson, has issued a special edition dealing with the state election laws, voting machines and paper ballots.

One contributor was Emily Paynter, who works for the Atlanta-based Voter Education Project at Tougaloo College. Miss Paynter, who is white and from Boston, has also produced motion pictures and color slide shows—using local people—to teach the basics of voting.

Moving quietly through several Delta communities was John Lewis, director of the voter education project and a founder and former head of S.N.C.C.

For a brief time today he reminisced about his first trip to Mississippi. "Ten years ago," he said, "I had no idea that in 10 years black people would be challenging just about the entire state."

U.S. to Send Observers

WASHINGTON, Nov. 1 (UPI) —Attorney General John N Mitchell ordered Federal ob-

Flonzie Goodloe, an elections commissioner in Madison County, teaching voting procedures

The New York Times/Thomas A. Johnson

*In Honor and Remembrance of some who paid
the ultimate price. They gave their lives for the cause of equality.*

IN MEMORIAM

Medgar Wiley Evers

July 2, 1925—June 12, 1963

John Fitzgerald Kennedy

May 29, 1917—November 23, 1964

Dr. Martin Luther King, Jr.

January 15, 1929--April 4, 1968

Robert Francis Kennedy

November 20, 1925—June 6, 1968

Chapter 6

Martin: As I Knew Him

In the early 1960's, James Meredith, a Black Mississippian, attempted to enter The University of Mississippi (Ole Miss), in North Mississippi. His attempt was denied. This act was yet another way of retaining the status quo. Cries for freedom were ringing throughout the country. Blacks everywhere were demonstrating their desire to become fully recognized citizens. It was time for all Americans to realize that the fetters, chains and shackles of racism, prejudice and discrimination had to become closed chapters in our history. It was time for America to, "Let Her People Go!!" We were no longer willing to remain second-class citizens.

In June 1966, in a single effort, James began the historic "Walk Against Fear." The 200-mile trek from Memphis to Jackson would prove Blacks were still courageous in spite of the many acts of violence. Just 18 miles south of Memphis, in

the little town of Hernando, MS, Mr. Meredith was struck by gunshot at the hands of a would-be-assassin. In support of him, large numbers of Blacks assembled in northern Mississippi to continue this symbolic, what had now became the Meredith March. Dr. Martin Luther King, Jr., was encouraged to lead the march. His presence was a show of solidarity along with other organizations.

As the march progressed down through the Mississippi Delta flatlands, scores of local Blacks joined with out-of-state whites, hand-in-hand. As the marchers neared Canton, I received a phone call from Dr.

Flonzie and Jessie Bernard

King asking if I could find housing and food for the more than 3,000 people who were converging on this small town. The marchers arrived in Canton on a hot Thursday mid-day afternoon. Father Luke, the Catholic Priest of the Holy Child Jesus Parish opened the gymnasium so that many could rest. Local Black townspeople also opened their homes as did many churches and many helped to prepare food for the marchers. Many local residents assisted with this huge undertaking. In spite of…, **We Did It!.**

Before the evening rally, several Blacks, including myself had the opportunity to meet with Dr. King and other nationally recognized organizers in the home of Mr. and Mr. George Washington, Sr.

Our discussion centered around such issues as how to strategically conduct the meeting, the mood of local whites, the fear of Blacks and the uncertainty of events. It was during this moving session that Martin talked openly about his death. He had a premonition that he would soon die a violent death. He challenged us to continue the struggle, when his inner feeling, would become a frightening reality. He challenged each of us to continue our involvement in spite of the difficult days ahead. At 6:00 p.m., we proceeded to the Holy Child Jesus gym to hear from this man who was small in stature, yet who was a great giant among us.

Friday morning, two major events were planned: 1). a march to the Madison County Courthouse; and, 2). the night freedom rally on the McNeal Elementary School grounds. Martin and Stokely Carmichael differed over the best approach. Martin emphasized non-violence, whereas Stokley's philosophy was more confrontational. The majority of us agreed to the non-violent approach. Much violence had been predicted and Martin was mindful of this and did not want local Blacks retaliated against unnecessarily after the march was over, when all of the National leaders and the press had gone back to their homes.

As we began to assemble for the march to the courthouse, tensions ran very high. This was the first time that local Blacks and whites had ever seen anything of this magnitude. We gathered by the thousands at the Mt. Zion Missionary Baptist Church.

Once we arrived at the courthouse, we were surrounded by many state troopers and local authorities. Most of us were frightened out of our wits, yet we knew the time had come for us to take a stand for truth, justice and equality.

It was my privilege and honor to introduce Martin on the steps of the Madison County Courthouse where, just a short time before, so many had been denied the right to register and hence to vote. There were many highway patrolmen positioned on the courthouse yard, some of whom had guns within inches of my back as I spoke. Despite his academic background, Martin spoke simply, with charismatic eloquence, where his enthusiastic message touched the hearts of all those assembled. Too see this "sea" of people has been forever etched in my mind.

His words, "We're on the move now, we can't stop now and non-violence will prevail", still ring clearly in my spirit, even today! He knew that was the better way as we could not out-shoot the officers.

Meredith March ~ Canton—June, 1966

To have had the opportunity to meet and march with so many great leaders and civil rights legends, will always be a momentous and historic moment in my career. I introduced Dr. Martin Luther King, Jr., on the same court house steps where many other Blacks including myself had been viciously turned away just for attempting to register and vote.

In addition to a rousing response from the crowd, a wonderful tension breaker occurred after I introduced Martin. An elderly Black gentleman yelled out from the crowd; "Whose daughter is that? Who raised that girl?" She sure can speak!!

My dad proudly shouted, "I did! She's my daughter!" Hearing my dad's response, my mom, (Mrs. Littie), responded, "We did, because part of the time, I didn't' know where you were!" This was so humorous, that everybody in hearing distance broke out into a big laugh.

When the rally was over, we marched back to the Mt. Zion Baptist Church arm-in-arm. The excitement and awe of being in Martin's presence is not easily forgotten. As the evening approached, great concern was generating about the strategies to be used for the night rally.

One major topic of dispute was whether or not we were going to "pitch the tent." Hoisting this huge tent would have allow hundreds of women and children to sleep on the school yard. The men were to sleep at the Holy Child Gymnasium. An order had been granted for a peaceful assembly on the school grounds, but not for the purpose of a sleep-in. Stokely's approach was to defy the local judge's order. Some of the local people made a make-shift stage from which our national leaders, Martin, Stokely, Floyd McKissick, Andrew Young, James Farmer and others spoke. Their speeches were stirring and fiery. As we sang many freedom songs, we were encircled by large numbers of state troopers who had been instructed to fire tear gas if there were the least effort to raise the tent. As Stokely spoke, he leaped from the make-shift stage to the ground chanting, louder and louder, over and over, *"We're gonna pitch the tent, we're gonna pitch the tent, because look at all of that Black Power that's out there!"* The term **Black Power** first used in the Delta, now in Canton, it became entrenched as a national Black slang. Its meaning was misinterpreted. It was meant to convey that as tax payers, we can use our Black power to vote, to become business owners, to become office holders, it was never meant to take on a negative connotation.

In a maze of mass confusion, the school ground was inundated with tear gas "cannons" filling the entire area with one big huge cloud of white choking smoke. The canisters flew in every direction, forcing hundreds of people being trampled to the ground, screaming and gasping for air. Patrolmen even stood on the roof of the school to also shoot down on us. As people managed to get up, they were knocked down again and again. Babies were crying, parents were trying to find their children and family members were trying to find other family members. There were some who were rushed to the local hospital with cuts, scrapes, cracked ribs and other injuries. But because of the racial climate, many were turned away.

Over all, I was blessed, I only sustained a sprained ankle and a scraped arm. Today, I wear physical scars from that experience. For many years, I would not wear short-sleeved clothing, because of the ugliness of the scars on my arm.

The next morning we met again in the Washington's home to discuss events of the previous evening..., that near death experience. Martin was able to calm the group by praying and asked if I would lead the song, "Oh Freedom". All of us joined in singing the song as it was one of his favorite songs of the movement. Then Martin said he wanted some soul food. I called mom and she cooked peas, fried chicken, mac and cheese, cornbread, a sweet potato pie and ice tea.

Mom fed Martin and a number of his comrades in our home. The dishes have been saved and when appropriate, they will be donated. After dinner I took Martin to visit the adult students at the STAR Program, my place of employment. There he gave them a rousing speech of encouragement. On Saturday morning, we began the 15-mile journey to Tougaloo College. From there, we proceeded to the State Capitol in Jackson where the march culminated with more than 16,000 people in attendance. This photo was taken at the STAR, Inc. I took this photo and several pictures of Martin, I regret I did not take one with him. The next time I was in his presence was at his funeral in Atlanta, GA, less than 2 years later. His premonition had come true.

Fast Forward:

The dishes that Dr. King ate out of at our home were donated to the MS Civil Rights Museum in 2018. They are now on display in honor of my mom.

Martin addressing the marchers at the Holy Child Jesus Catholic Gym in June, 1966.

This is a copy of more than 20,000 leaflets circulated announcing the March and Freedom Rally.

It's important for me to revisit the Lorraine Motel in Memphis. On a frequent basis, I find myself walking the grounds, looking at Martin's room and actually viewing the spot where "The Dreamer" was killed.

This experience is not only energizing, but it reminds me of the 1966 conversation he shared about his death. It strengthens my resolve that we must never let go of the dream. I'm reminded that the struggle is not over, in spite of many gains which have been made in Mississippi.

The City of Memphis purchased this facility which houses much of the civil rights memorabilia during Martin's visit. This National Civil Rights Museum has been dedicated and pays tribute to those who were a part of Martin's struggle.

I never saw Martin alive again. In April, 1968, I found myself in Atlanta with many thousands, including a number of Cantonians, paying our final respects to him. In writing this book twenty-six years later, (1968-1994), I often wonder when did everybody get home, how they got there, how long were their journeys, would our paths ever cross again? Many paths have crossed, some haven't.

We must never let go of Martin's dream!

The Lorraine Motel ~ Memphis, TN—1991

The Lorraine Motel, June 1964

The wreath still hangs on the door of Martins' room. These cars were used to escort him to the hotel from the airport the night before his assassination. They are still parked in the same spot, more than 30 years later. On a regular basis, the cars are restored to their original look.

This is the spot where the assassin stood to kill Martin. This spot is located across the street from the Motel.

Chapter 7

Saluting My Sistah's:
Phenomenal Women of Courage

There is a unique bond that only "Sistah's" share. As Sistah's, we are mothers, wives, aunts, grandmothers, nieces, friends and strong anchors. Women have always possessed the creative ability to care for the home, to make a way when there seemed to be no way, to watch the backs of our brothers, and provide general nurturing for our families. We are at our best when we accept these challenges in stride, give our best and move on to the next level. This is not to say that men have not played their part, because they too have paid a heavy price for freedom.

This segment is written to pay tribute to the many women who have been and are a part of my life. They have allowed me to learn from them. I've seen over the years, a tremendous amount of wisdom, courage, ingenuity, warm and caring spirits emanating from this group. So many women have had a major impact on my life. Several are now deceased. Ms. Ethel Lucille Nichols, elementary school secretary and Mt. Zion Missionary Baptist Church choir leader. She furthered my music endeavors and was truly my mentor. She had a way of walking that I and others tried to emulate. Mrs. Daisy Powell and Mrs. Willie Harris helped me to ensure that my children had balanced meals when I had to work late or travel out of town. My mom's sister, Aunt Zettie, was also a second mother to me. Her soft natured way inspired me in many areas of my life. My dad's sister, Aunt Precious, had a quiet unassuming manner of demonstrating strong love and compassion. She often referred to me as the daughter she never had. Mrs. Marian "Pete" Robinson not only shared her musical talents with me, but was well known in the Canton civil rights and church community. She could play any song!

Our eldest family member, Cousin Ida, taught me how to create a one-pot meal using a soup bone, potatoes and vegetables. Each time I cook a pot of soup or stew, I attempt to flavor it as she did. I have not yet achieved that special flavor. Mrs. Cora Jean Watkins, Aunt Cora as my children call her, and Mrs. Annie Lou Warnsley, (Auntie), both cared for my children from time to time when I had to work unusual hours. I shall always cherish the love and friendship of Mother Helene Goodloe. She has been an ideal grandmother to my children and an inspiration and second mother to me.

So many of my friends are now living in various parts of the country. Others are now deceased, I miss them beyond words can ever express.

Mrs. Mamie "Dolly" Marshall Robinson and Mrs. Monette Devine Watts have been two of my long-time best friends since the second grade.

From an historical perspective, we have stood on the strength of many women including: Sisters' Rosa Parks, Fannie Lou Hamer, Harriet Tubman, Sojourner Truth, Ida B. Wells, Mary McLeod Bethune, Shirley Chisholm, Victoria Gray, Dorothy Height, C. DeLores Tucker, Biddy Mason, Ella Josephine Baker and so many others. As each of these women shaped the course of history, they did so without trying. They were motivated by what was right and were never concerned about who would ultimately get the credit. We have much to thank them for.

My soul-mate, Mrs. Bertha Younger Walwyn from Yazoo City, lived with us when I was twelve. She came to Canton to find work. She convinced Mom to let me wear my first pair of stockings. I was almost thirteen. We often chuckle about Mom's reaction. We are as close today, if not closer, as we were during those *Younger* years. I am grateful also for the friendship of Ms. Lillian Louie who shared what I know today about Medgar Evers' life. Mrs. Lillian Butler was, and continues to be an anchor for me since my days of working in the Washington, DC area. My sister-in-law, Mrs. Mary J. Brown, the Wright daughters-in-law, Sister "T" and Mrs. Annie Devine, have all encouraged me to share with others my varied experiences. A special salute to my mom's best friend, Mrs. Lou Doris Garrett, (Cousin Lou), for being a special friend to me also. Mrs. Dorothy Stewart had the vision to organize Women For Progress, Inc., (WFP), organized in 1978 as a state-wide organization. This group addresses the stresses of teen pregnancy, educational opportunities, social, political and a myriad of community issues. There are many, many more women who are a part of me, I appreciate all of you.

Another great group of local women endeared themselves to me. These phenomenal women of courage were most often referred to as "The Mattie Girls." They included: Mrs. Betty Robinson, Mrs. Clarice Coney, Ms. Mary Nell Whisenton, Ms. Pearl Nichols, Mrs. Sarah Singleton and Ms. Jewel Williams. Mattie's was a safe haven, a place of refuge for all of us. The common thread that kept us together was, "we were working for the future of all our children."

Each of us had strong role models to follow. Our mothers instilled in each of us the desire to excel and succeed. We were taught from little girls that we were as good as anyone and we should never be ashamed of who we were. We were reassured that as long as we did what was right, that right would follow us. That counsel became our standard for living. Most of all, I thank my mom for being steadfast in her training of me and so many other young women in Canton who called her "mom" as a way of showing their love for her. The list is endless. Enduring love never fails.

The ideas for many community activities originated from this group. In addition to our hard work, each Sistah freely gave of their talents, gifts and skills. We developed and implemented many program initiatives through community organizations, such as Head Start, STAR, Inc., COFO, SNCC, NAACP, MFDP, SCLC, MCUP, The Bethune Day Care Center, and other initiatives. Our concern was not for ourselves, but to provide opportunities not only for our children, but for children of surrounding communities. We were involved daily in disseminating leaflets, going to meetings, going to church, working with the school children, trying to get head-start funded, trying to organize community boards, addressing a multiplicity of community problems, preparing for mass mailings, and getting out the vote on election day. Our work never ended.

All we wanted to know was where and what time the planning meetings were. Most often, the meetings were in my home on Boyd Street. Many times we did not have enough money among all of us to buy a loaf of bread or a bottle of juice, but we made it. My Sistah's would bring their children to our meetings. Each person would bring something to share: a package of kool-aid, hot-dogs, eggs, margarine or rice. We cooked, fed our children and began our work, which could last into the night.

They often tease me about the time when Representative John Conyers came to Canton and I was going to barbecue ribs because we were feeding him in my home. Betty came over and saw the ribs in a Dutch oven in the oven. She laughed at me so hard, telling me that the ribs would never get done in that deep pot. She put them on a cookie sheet and baked them as they should be. Even though I was a good cook, I could not barbecue.

We often laugh about another time when we were meeting and another girlfriend called to ask if she could join us. I proceeded to tell her to come over, as we were involved in a work session. I also welcomed her to eat with us because I assured her, "We have plenty." My Sistah's reminded me on that day, we only had one piece of meat, two eggs, and a tablespoon of margarine. That was all. We pooled our pennies and bought and prepared food for the person who was coming. It was our constancy and our willingness to share what we had with each other that kept us on course. These women put their lives on the line everyday in spite of their husbands being intimidated, forced out and even fired from their jobs. These tremendous women of courage are still leading the way in Canton for the many children who are yet to come. They worked diligently not only during my campaign, but have continued to work in many community endeavors. I remember so well the day that Dr. King was assassinated, April 4, 1968. In an earlier meeting with him in 1966, he predicted his violent death. I received a call from activist Jewel that the students had walked out of Canton High School, they were heading down town and that the sheriff's office had been called to stop them.

Immediately after Jewel's call, I received a frantic call from the school principal asking for help. He shared with me that the students wanted to have a meeting in the school gymnasium and they wanted to call some of us in to meet with them. He wanted to personally accommodate their request; however, he had no authority to permit the meeting on the school campus. A flurry of frantic calls and actions followed. Canton is a small town and the word spread quickly that the students had walked out of school and were recklessly out of control.

We were unsure of the student's location. We knew we had to get to these young people before the law enforcement officials found them. Jewel also told me where she believed the students were headed. They were on their way downtown to hold "their rally" at the Madison County Court House. We knew that to be a dangerous move.

I jumped into my car and tried to head them off. I found them walking down Frost Street and positioned my car to block them. By that time a number of adults had arrived, and were beginning to disperse themselves throughout the angry crowd. It was most reassuring to see so many courageous women and men who were putting their lives at risk to reach out and help calm our angry children.

We knew a crisis was at hand. There must have been more than 1200 students. They were shouting; they were angry; they were crying and were completely out of control.

The "Mattie" Girls

Jewel Williams, Flonzie, Clarice Coney, Betty Robinson and Mary Whisenton. We lovingly remember Sarah Singleton and Clarice Coney

I stood on top of my car to try and get their attention. Just down the hill were city and county law enforcement officials, outfitted in riot gear with their AR 15's and other weapons drawn. The mood in the county at that time was extremely tense. We were convinced that our children were going to be hurt or even killed had we not reached them.

Amazingly, in the midst of this trauma, God intervened. I fell from the top of my car into a muddy ditch! The mood changed immediately. A couple of young people ran to assist me. When they discovered I was not injured, just covered with mud, the entire group collapsed into laughter. We were then able to redirect their energies. The teaching that, "God works in mysterious ways", became real through that incident.

They began to listen to us and eventually allowed us to gain control. The students wanted to march up to the court house and hold a rally in the courtyard. In those days, marchers had to receive a written permit from the city to assemble on government property. After much discussion, we talked them into peacefully marching to the Mt. Zion Missionary Baptist Church which was close by and where they were allowed to cry, express themselves and get all of their emotions out without any bloodshed. Reverend P. F. Parker, Pastor and Reverend Bennie Luckett came and prayed with the children. We all sang freedom songs. They left the church peacefully and returned home; where most were in the care of their parents.

From this group of Women of Courage, Mrs. Betty Robinson became the first Black female to be appointed as Deputy Clerk for the Madison County Justice Court. Mrs. Annie Pearl Nichols pursued her career in the nursing profession. Mrs. Sarah Singleton prepared herself to educate children and staff in the Head Start effort. Mrs. Mary Nell Whisenton became a state officer with the Mississippi Parent Teacher Association. Mrs. Clarice Coney became a State staff person with Head Start. Mrs. Jewel Williams became the first Black Alderwoman for the City of Canton. Mrs. Mamie Chinn became Canton's first Black female judge.

Our friendship has remained strong through the years. I salute the many Sistah's who are continuing to make Canton a better place for all.

In recalling their strength, I'm reminded of Sojourner Truth's dramatic presentation of, "*Ain't I A Woman!*". in part, "*Now you mean to tell me 'dat if one woman turned dis wor'l upside down, you mean to tell me 'dat all 'dese women out heah can't turn 'dis wor'l right-side up... A'int I A Woman?*"(May 29, 1851)

These and many more are Phenomenal Women of Courage!

Part IV
Personal Reflections on Moving Ahead

After spending many hours in deep concentration and reflection about the importance of this writing experience, it's only fitting and proper that this segment place in perspective the concept of "Moving Ahead." As I attempt to capture this concept, there are three major issues I'd like to address:

1. Looking at Who We Are
2. Healing the Land
3. Revisiting the City of Canton: Summary Interviews:
   The Honorable Mayor Sidney Runnels: 1978—1994
   The Honorable Mayor Alice M. Scott: 1994—2002

My active involvement in Canton continued through 1973, when my family and I moved to Jackson. Early in 1974, I was appointed by the United States Equal Employment Opportunity Commission (EEOC), as an Investigator of job discrimination complaints. My appointment allowed me to continue the work I had begun in Canton. I was both pleased and excited. It allowed me to expand my skills in the area of employment opportunity for minorities and to champion the cause of my sisters and brothers who were experiencing employment discrimination in a variety of forms. As an investigator, my area of responsibility included the State of Mississippi. In addition to my official capacity as an Investigator for the EEOC, I joined the Collective Bargaining Unit of the American Federation of Government Employees (AFGE) AFL-CIO, Local 3599. I was immediately elected as Treasurer, an Executive Board Position. I served the Union in various capacities, including that of President from 1982-1989. I was responsible for an eight state Collective Bargaining area along with national assignments. Local 3599 encompassed the states of Mississippi, Alabama, Georgia, North Carolina, South Carolina, Kentucky, Tennessee, and Florida. National negotiations were held in Washington, DC and New York City. I also became Vice-President of the National Council of EEOC Locals #216, the parent organization, headquartered in New York City. We understood that our allegiance was to our employees and I believe we fulfilled that mission with integrity, equality and competence. These countless experiences enhanced my personal and professional growth and development. Many long-standing friendships were cultivated and still remain. I'm still called upon periodically to give voice to collective bargaining issues and the benefits of being an organized group of individuals.

Many of my colleagues in the EEOC received their initial training as I did, as activists in the civil rights movement. Our community work enabled us to assist thousands of Mississippians and many others across the country, who had been victims of workplace discrimination.

Shortly after moving to Jackson in 1974, my son, Ed, Jr., went to the neighborhood park to play softball. He was about 13 years old. The ball park was filled with white boys his own age. He went to the gate to ask to become a member of the team. He was asked by the coach to leave because he could not play in that park. Ed came and told me what had happened. After making a few telephone calls, I found that the City of Jackson was paying the coaches, the utility bills and buying their uniforms. A number of efforts were made to rectify the situation, all to no avail. With the assistance of Attorney George Bradley, we filed legal action against the City of Jackson. This lawsuit resulted in the Lake Hico Park being opened to all citizens. I realized that I could not continue to take on every battle. That was not my intention. However, my advocacy skills had to be used in this instance. My own child was involved. I could not back away. Today, it is a good feeling to visit and see people of all races, ethnicities and backgrounds enjoying this "once white only" recreational facility.

In the years since Jackson, I have traveled in and out of the State of Mississippi, in and out of the City of Canton. I have seen many positive changes. I understand that all of my goals and dreams have not been fully realized, but I remain hopeful and optimistic as I continue to work, collaborate, and network with other people, other organizations throughout my home city, around the state and around the nation. The opportunity to look back, move ahead and share some of my life experiences reminds me of my commitment to my Creator. I believe this book is a part of my commission; hence I will continue to serve as long as I can. As a result of this commitment, I have established the *Flonzie B. Wright Scholarship Foundation.* It is my vision that this effort will be a means of providing scholarship support and opportunities to as many as possible.

In great part, there was another experience which prepared me for services to others. In the mid-sixties when the Office of Economic Opportunity funded community programs, each agency had an EEO (Equal Employment Officer). That included Head-Start, STAR, Inc., and other programs. The majority of the Officers were African American. When employees brought complaints to our attention, we were responsible for negotiating a satisfactory resolution with our respective agencies. Little did any of us know that we were being prepared for a greater service to others.

There is a place for each of us as we choose to be involved in the continuous struggle for the rights of all our citizens. We shall all move ahead with pride, with unity and with a sense of responsibility.

Chapter 1

Validating the "African-ness" In Me

It was not too long ago, when I remember that we Americans of African descent, were often hesitant to validate our African roots. Now as African Americans, we are proudly proclaiming our cultural heritage in many ways. One observable example of the creative ingenuity of our people is in the wearing of African attire. The idea of Africa as our homeland is becoming more widely known and accepted. What a creative and beautiful artful display of culture.

It is important to remember our ancestors who were uprooted from Africa and brought to a country they could not call their own. When I think of those who died from all forms of negligence, murder and suicide, I am proud to be linked with a people who have withstood so many injustices and paid so many dues. I am proud to be linked with the strength of Nelson Mandela. Mr. Mandela spent 28 years in prison because he would not compromise his principles. He became President of South Africa in 1994, three years after his release from prison. He is a clear example of the meaning of character, morality, and pride. We are descendants of Kings and Queens.

There is clearly supported evidence that man's roots are in Africa. This evidence is affirmed in the Bible. It is clear to me from studying the Bible that the Garden of Eden is in Africa. Genesis 2:13 describes that the four rivers ran out of the Garden and where they ended. It is clear that one of the rivers ended in Ethiopia--in Eastern Africa.

As we read through the Bible, I am convinced that a number of people were of color or even Black. I feel that if man was created from the dust of the ground, he had to have been a man of color.

We must teach our young people of their importance. This can best be done through sharing our history and our legacy. We must never forget those thousands of slaves who departed from the "Door of No Return" in Senegal, Africa, never to see our homeland ever again. We must remember that it was the African culture which taught European Americans many of its current skills. We must share the stories that our people have value. No one is excluded, we are all special people.

We need to also teach our children the principles as well as the meaning of Kwanzaa; an African-American holiday celebration that begins on December 26th and ends January 1st. Founded in 1966 by Dr. Maulana Karenga, "the holiday is a time of ingathering for African-Americans to celebrate our history."

The seven principles of **Kwanzaa:**

Imani (i-ma-ni), faith
Kujichagulia (ku-ji-cha-gu-lia), self determination
Kuumba (ku-um-ba), creativity
Nia (ni-a), purpose
Ujamaa (u-ja-ma),cooperative economics
Ujima (u-ji-ma), collective work and responsibility
Umoja (u-mo-ja), unity

Clothing is represented as follows:

buba (bu-ba), elegant gown or robe
busita (bu-su-ti), a robe with scarf at the waist
dashiki (da-shi-ki) a loosely fitting shirt for boys and men ; a
loosely fitting blouse for girls or women
gele (ge-le), a head wrap
kanzu (kan-zu), a robe for men

Ritual Symbols of Kwanzaa:

bendera (ben-de-ra), flag
kikombe (ki-kom-be), a cup
kikombe cha umoja (ki-kom-be- cha- u-mo-ja), unity cup
kinara (ki-na-ra), candle holder
mazoa (ma-zo-a), crops
mkeka (m-ke-ka), mat
mishumaa (mi-shu-ma-a), candles
mishumaa saba (mi-shu-ma-a sa-ba), seven candles
Vibunzi (vi-bun-zi), ears of corn
Zawadi (za-wa-di), gift or gifts

Swahili Greetings:

habari gani (ha-ba-ri ga-ni), what's the news?
Kwanzaa yenu iwe heri (kwan-za ye-nu i-we he-ri),
Happy Kwanzaa

Aluta Continua - The struggle continues

Understanding the

Legacy of Queen Nefertiti

According to the Egyptian Museum in West Berlin, we do not know the background of Akhenaten's chief queen, Nefertiti. One school of thought is that at one time scholars believed that she was a princess from Naharin: the meaning of her name, "A beautiful woman arrives", seems to support this school of thought.

It seems likely that she came from an influential military family which was closely related to the royal family over many generations. Perhaps these connections began with the marriage of Amosis, the SHEBA founder of the Eighteenth Dynasty, to the heiress of the Hyksos, king in Lower Egypt. It is thought that Nefertiti was the niece of Tiye, the queen of Amenophis III, and the granddaughter of Mutemwiya, the mother of Amenophis. These women had been chief queens, as Nefertiti was.

She is known as the goddess of love and beauty. When we wear her symbols, let's remember the strength of this woman who ruled her country for many years. Let's be proud to wear her clothes, sing her songs, laugh her laugh, walk her walk, talk her talk. Nefertiti--a great, beautiful, Egyptian African Queen. As women of African descent, we wear her symbols proudly.

The African Pledge

WE are An African People...

WE will remember the humanity, glory and sufferings of our Ancestors, and honor the struggle of our Elders...

WE will strive to bring new values, and new life to our people;

WE will have peace, and harmony among us.

WE will be loving, sharing and creative.

WE will work, study and listen;
    so **WE** may learn, learn so **WE** may teach

WE will cultivate self-reliance.

WE will struggle and resurrect and unify our homeland;

WE will raise many children for our nation...

WE will have discipline, patience, devotion and courage;

WE will live as models, to provide new direction for our people...

WE will be free and self determining;

WE are African People,

WE will win, **WE** will win, **WE** will win...

(This writing was shared by Mrs. Dorothy Steward, Founder of Women For Progress, Inc. This presentation was made at the 1992 Annual Kwanzaa Celebration of the Canton Chapter of Women for Progress, Inc.

Author Unknown

Fast Forward: : Mrs. Dorothy Stewart

Samuel passed in July, 2018

Reflecting on my African Heritage

1994

Chapter 2

Heal The Land

In recent years, we have witnessed an erosion of the values and principles that were taught by our fore-parents. All kinds of negative behaviors have emerged in our community. At one time we worried about equal jobs, equal housing opportunities, equal access to public accommodation, voting rights, etc. Today our worries are drive-by shootings, muggings, joy killings, drug use and abuse and other kinds of sordid, unjustifiable acts. For years, we have complained about the effects of institutionalized racism. Now, in far too many instances, we practice in the extreme what we complained about. <u>We must recommit ourselves to the safety of all of us.</u>

This nation must be healed. We must get back to the values of God and family. 2nd Chronicles: Chapter 7, Verse 14, teaches that, *"If my people, which are called by my name shall humble themselves, and pray, and seek my face, and turn from their wicked ways; then will I hear from heaven, and will forgive their sin, and I will heal the land."*

Today, we live in a "throw away society". We throw away our elderly, we throw away our children, we throw away our school systems, we throw away our self-inherent values and principles, we throw away our poor. The homeless, the helpless and the needy experience hopelessness because we do not want to know about or acknowledge their poverty. If we pretend that these unpleasant circumstances do not exist, then we are not obliged to take any corrective action. If we refuse ownership of the problem, we do not have to extend ourselves. We must acknowledge that these are our problems and we can and must find ways to solve them.

We have always been a people of hope. Hope can simply be defined as an expectation of something to come. Perhaps Webster may have another meaning, but in layman's terms, it means we anticipate something because of a belief. If we believe that we can collectively or individually, "Heal the Land", then we possess the ability to make an impact. If we are not willing to extend ourselves, then there is no hope.

Hope is what sustained our fore-parents as they built our country. Hope has inspired us to make this nation the best it can be. I hope for a better day, I hope America never forsakes its people. I hope that there will be no homelessness in this country. I hope for full employment. I hope we will stop "trashing our babies." No child should go to bed hungry in our country. All elderly persons should have proper medical and health care.

I believe better neighborhoods build better societies. I believe better neighborhoods existed when we acknowledged prayer in our public school system. I believe we had better neighborhoods when neighbors were not afraid to assist with the rearing of neighborhood children. I believe our neighborhoods were better when we really cared about each other. I believe we had better neighborhoods when neighbors could drop by another neighbor's house and get a meal. I remember when people did not have to lock doors they could leave home and not be afraid for their safety. My, how neighborhoods have changed.

It is my opinion that the mission of the Black Church is two-fold: 1). that of nurturing the soul; and, 2). providing a safe haven for its people. My experiences in growing up in southern churches were positive. Souls were comforted, spiritual guidance was provided and all kinds of needs were met. Our Elders played a major role in our development.

Every church had a Mother Susie, a Sister Mary or a Brother John. Sister Mary took the hungry home for a good meal after church. Mother Susie taught sewing so that clothing would be available for the needy. Brother John brought a bag of sweet potatoes and greens from his field and his wife sent along a pie or sweet bread. People in the church took time with children to train and teach them life-long lessons and values.

In my memory, the pastor of the church visited his members and knew the needs of each of his parishioners. He knew all of the family members by name and served to inspire the husband/father in the home to keep his family together in church. He could tell you something special about each member in the church. My overall concern is that we have gotten too far away from the reasons why our parents and fore-parents established our churches. Our churches must remain places of refuge and places of hope, many still are.

We must restore some of the values which bring hope. I remain hopeful that if we prioritize our personal values, this will have a domino effect that will continue to spill over into our society. We must heal the land!

We must never forget the challenges and legacies' of our ancestors. Their priorities were always the welfare of their families and passing those values on to their children, grandchildren, great-grandchildren and all in future generations to come. When I contemplate the life of the ol' folks and how they made it in spite of, I can't help but to do all that I can to teach this to future generations. They must know who we are and how we got to where we are today. I can see our ancestors working from sun-up to sun-down, just to make a few dollars. Compared to where we are today, there is simply **NO** comparison.

Chapter 3

"Canton ~ Then and Now"

Part I

The Honorable Mayor Sidney Runnels, April 4, 1994

In writing the closing Chapter of *Looking Back To Move Ahead,* many hours have been dedicated to try and simplify the concept of the book's title. We have spent precious time examining and re-examining the true meaning and purpose of this concept.

I began writing this book in my mind, in the early 70's. Not being an Author presented quite a challenge. Once I began the writing experience, endless hours were spent digging through many boxes of written materials and examining hundreds of photographs. Being the "pack-rat" that I am, I was amazed as I plowed through many valuable mementos, how much information I had collected over the years.

April 4, 1994
Mayor Sidney Runnels - Canton, Mississippi

As we prepare to "Move Ahead", I asked then current Mayor Sidney Runnels to share his views on this concept. He graciously accepted the invitation. Our views about Canton are shared in summary form.

SUMMARY STATEM ENT BY MAYOR RUNNELS:

We've come a long way. We come from a community that's got a lot of heart. People don't mind letting you know how they feel, with a hug, with a smile. If I could leave a legacy about the City of Canton, I'd like to refer to one of my favorite shows, "The Wizard of Oz." As Dorothy says, "There's no place like home." I am saying, there is no place like Canton. I don't see race as we were raised. I don't like that. I get very disturbed. We have four races; North, South, East and West. We don't have races, we have people. You cannot run a city if you come in with a biased racial attitude. I am the mayor for everybody.

If I don't live that, how can I ask others to do likewise. When I make a decision, then I can lie down at night and feel good about it. There are times when people don't always agree with me. My decisions are made upon what is fair for the citizens of this city. I never vote on an issue unless there is a tie vote.

Philosophically, I am guided by Galatians 6:4. In paraphrase, I'm instructed to do the very best that I can and don't worry about being compared to someone else. God made us all as individuals. When we come to that final day of judgment, He's not going to compare me with anyone else. I have to stand for myself. We are all God's children. I complement you on your courage in letting your story be told. I am quite excited about it. I am pleased that you have never forgotten Canton.

SUMMARY STATEMENT BY BROWN-WRIGHT:

Canton is my home. I've traveled quite extensively, but I found myself always coming back to Canton. I have a special affinity for Canton, the Blacks, the Whites, the elderly, the young. I grew up in a home where my parents did not teach racial hatred. I knew nothing about racism or segregation. We were taught to respect and love everybody for who they were. As we look at *Canton - Then and Now,* I can see many positive changes since the 60's. The thrust of the civil rights movement was that; families would be stronger, our cities would be better and our children would have a better opportunity to grow and thrive in a healthy manner.

It's my hope and prayer that the *Flonzie B. Wright Scholarship Foundation* will further those thrusts. If this effort helps only one child or one family, then the effort has been worth it. If one child can buy a book or buy a bag of pencils, this small effort will help. We need to build stronger families. We need to build stronger communities. **We do not need to build bigger jails.** We can make this city, the state of Mississippi and this nation a better place for all people. **LET's JUST DO IT!**

"Canton ~ Then and Now"

Part II

The Honorable Alice M. Scott, Mayor, September 1999

Subsequent to publishing this work in 1994, my hometown of Canton elected as mayor an individual whom I have known for many years. I thought it would be fitting and proper to also ask her for her views and comments about our hometown.

In 1999, the Millennium Edition and sixth printing of *Looking Back To Move Ahead* became a best seller. It is important to me that the reader has an appreciation for how Canton has changed and to grasp a current perspective of those changes.

That same year, Mayor Alice M. Scott provided such an opportunity for me to share how she feels about the growth and development of my hometown, Canton, Mississippi.

Many changes have occurred over the past five years, Mayor Alice M. Scott recalls a few... In the fall of 1994, the citizens of Canton voiced their desires when they elected me as their leader. I am a long-time resident of Canton and have always worked for the betterment of all citizens. I am honored to wear the title, "Mayor of all the People." We are twenty miles north of the Capitol City of Jackson. It is an historic community that is over one hundred and sixty years old and boasts of architectural beauty, warmth and grace. This town is a real community where neighbors care about neighbors, businesses enhance business and the rewards are realized by economic and positive growth.

Upon taking office, my focus was directed on some of the following issues: *Education and Improved Facilities, Equality in Police & Fire Protection, Year Round Parks and Recreation Programs, Comprehensive Flood & Drainage Plan, Economic Development and New Industry, Housing, Street Improvement and Improved Race Relations.*

Because of the strong leadership of dedicated team members, many of these and other goals have been realized. As we prepare for the next generation, those success stories are being celebrated as follows:

New and Existing Industries, New Businesses, New State of the Art High School and Performing Arts Center, New Shopping Complex, Multicultural Museum, Increased Tourism and Film Industry, New Housing and Residential Subdivisions, Senior Assisted Living Facility for Retirees, and New and Improved Walking Parks and Recreational Facilities. Our vision continues for a more progressive Canton.

Many persons who reside outside of the State of Mississippi may perceive the South in a negative manner. Historically, that was the case. Today, I can say with confidence that many of the old stigmas and ism's have been eradicated. I applaud all citizens for doing their part to ensure that we never return to those days again. Anyone can hate..., but it takes a special person to breakthrough those barriers and accentuate the positive. I am pleased to say that our citizens have made every effort to promote our city in the most positive manner possible.

We have been fortunate to have had three major movies filmed in Canton:" *A Time to Kill, My Dog Skip and O' Brother, Where Art Thou?"* Other productions are being discussed.

Each year, citizens look forward to two major events: The Canton Flea Market held in May and October which attracts more than 50,000 persons and the Canton Gospel Fest featuring a Homecoming for the nationally acclaimed, Canton Spirituals.

Our city is filled with many stories which need to be told. I am personally pleased to be a part of this exciting Millennium Edition of Flonzie's publication. Since the early 1960's she has been a trailblazer at times when it was not popular for African Americans and Women in particular to be on the cutting edge of change. I am standing where I am today in great part because of Flonzie's steadfastness. It was her election to the Board of Election Commissioners in 1968 that formed the foundation for many more to follow. As a result of her courageous spirit, years later, I also was elected to that same board.

We remember those who stood in the face of many adversities so that those of us who occupy a variety of elected and appointed positions in Canton can do so with dignity and pride. Many Cantonians risked their lives daily so that we can fully realize the American dream of our fore-parents.

I also applaud the efforts of the Scholarship Foundation which has assisted many Canton students with scholarship opportunities. Flonzie's giving spirit continues to teach each of us how to give..., give so we may receive. Canton stands with her in telling her story, we are proud that she continues to promote our city in a positive light.

In Memory of my Grandparents:

Dad's Parents: **Mr. & Mrs. Robert (Frances) Brown**

Mom's Parents: **Mr. & Mrs. Bozie (Flonzie) Dawson**

My Family: Syd, Dad, Mom, me and Frank, Jr.